Welcome to Issue Seven

Heroes and Zeros

C000140431

XTB stands for **eXplore The Bible**.

Read a bit of the Bible each day and...
- Zoom in on **Mark** to meet Jesus, the promised King.
- Check out **Judges**—the book of heroes and zeros!
- Meet King David's great grandmother in the book of **Ruth**.

Are you ready to explore the Bible? Fill in the bookmark...
...then turn over the page to start exploring with XTB!

Sometimes I'm called

.... (nickname)

My birthday is

....

My age is

....

My hero is...

Table Talk FOR FAMILIES

Look out for **Table Talk** — a book to help children and adults explore the Bible together. It can be used by:
- Families
- One adult with one child
- Children's leaders with their groups
- Any other way you want to try

Table Talk uses the same Bible passages as XTB so that they can be used together if wanted. You can buy Table Talk from your local Good Book Company website:
UK: www.thegoodbook.co.uk • North America: www.thegoodbook.com
Australia: www.thegoodbook.com.au • New Zealand: www.thegoodbook.co.nz

OLD TESTAMENT	NEW TESTAMENT
Genesis	Matthew
Exodus	**Mark**
Leviticus	Luke
Numbers	John
Deuteronomy	Acts
Joshua	Romans
Judges	1 Corinthians
Ruth	2 Corinthians
1 Samuel	Galatians
2 Samuel	Ephesians
1 Kings	Philippians
2 Kings	Colossians
1 Chronicles	1 Thessalonians
2 Chronicles	2 Thessalonians
Ezra	1 Timothy
Nehemiah	2 Timothy
Esther	Titus
Job	Philemon
Psalms	Hebrews
Proverbs	James
Ecclesiastes	1 Peter
Song of Solomon	2 Peter
Isaiah	1 John
Jeremiah	2 John
Lamentations	3 John
Ezekiel	Jude
Daniel	Revelation
Hosea	
Joel	
Amos	
Obadiah	
Jonah	
Micah	
Nahum	
Habakkuk	
Zephaniah	
Haggai	
Zechariah	
Malachi	

How to find your way around the Bible...

Look out for the **READ** sign.
It tells you what Bible bit to read.

READ
Mark 8v27-30

So, if the notes say... READ Mark 8v27-30
...this means chapter 8 and verses 27 to 30
...and this is how you find it.

Use the **Contents** page in your Bible to find where Mark begins

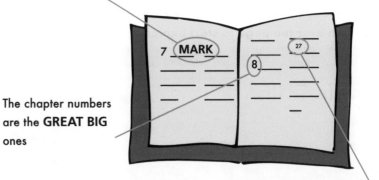

The chapter numbers are the **GREAT BIG** ones

7 MARK   8   27

The verse numbers are the tiny ones!

Oops! Keep getting lost?
Cut out this bookmark and use it to keep your place.

How to use xtb

1  Find a time and place when you can read the Bible each day.

2  Get your Bible, a pencil and your XTB notes.

3  Ask God to help you to understand what you read.

4  Read today's XTB page and Bible bit.

5 Pray about what you have read and learned.

6  If you can, talk to an adult or a friend about what you've learned.

XTB Heroes and Zeros

Who are the Heroes? And who are Zeros?

Are you ready to find out? Then hurry on to Day 1.

The words below are written in the **Greek** and **Hebrew** languages. *Crack the code to see what they say.*

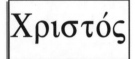

_____ _____ _____ _____ _____ _____

This is Greek. Mark wrote his book about Jesus in Greek.

_____ _____ _____ _____ _____ _____ _____

This is Hebrew. It is read <u>backwards</u>, from right to left.

Did you know?

The Bible wasn't written in English! Most of the <u>Old Testament</u> was written in **Hebrew**. A tiny bit was written in another language, called **Aramaic**. The <u>New Testament</u> was all written in **Greek**.

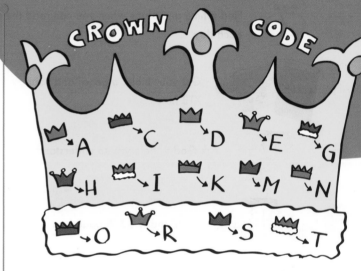

CROWN CODE

A → C → D → E → G
H → I → K → M → N
O → R → S → T

Christ and Messiah are actually the <u>same</u> word, but in <u>different</u> languages. *Do some more code-cracking to see what they mean.*

_ _ _ _ , _ _ _ _ _ _ _ _ _

Find out more on the next page.

KING JESUS

Mark's book is all about King Jesus. It's divided into two halves:

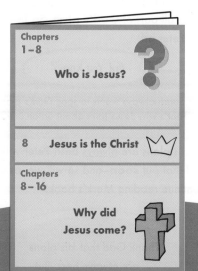

Chapters 1–8

Who is Jesus?

8 Jesus is the Christ

Chapters 8–16

Why did Jesus come?

We read the <u>first half</u> in Issues Five and Six of *XTB*. It's about **who** Jesus is. Now it's time to start the <u>second half</u> of Mark's book, to see **why** Jesus came.

READ
Mark 8v27-30

People had plenty of ideas about Jesus. Some thought He was *John the Baptist*, come back to life. Others thought He was *Elijah*, or one of the other prophets (God's messengers).

But what did **Peter** say? (v29)

You are the

Peter was right!
Jesus is the **Christ** (Messiah)
—He is *God's chosen King!*

What does Jesus tell His disciples <u>not</u> to do? (v30)
a) Not to listen to Peter.
b) Not to tell anyone who Jesus is.
c) Not to do handstands.

Jesus says they are not to tell people who He is—because they don't <u>understand</u> yet. They don't know what sort of King Jesus is going to be.

That's what the second half of Mark's book is about. *And that's what we'll start finding out about tomorrow...*

PRAY

Dear God, please help me to learn more about King Jesus and why He came as I read Mark's book. Amen

THE KING WHO CAME TO DIE

 Mark 8v31-33

 Ahem! Pay attention! Today's reading has some tricky terms in it, and you need to know what they mean...

Tricky Terms
- Son of Man—a name for Jesus.
- Elders, Chief Priests and Teachers of the Law—religious leaders.
- To rebuke—to tell off.
- Satan—the devil.

Peter and the other disciples have just discovered **who** Jesus is. He's the *Christ*. He's God's chosen King! But He's <u>not</u> the sort of King they're expecting...

READ
Mark 8v31-33

Spot the Difference *There are five to spot.*

What did Jesus say would happen to Him? (v31) *Fill in the gaps.*

reject
three
suffer
killed

- He would s_____.
- The religious leaders would r_____ Him.
- He would be k_____.
- After t_____ days He would come back to life.

Was Peter pleased by what Jesus said? (v32) **Yes / No**

Peter was horrified! Surely Jesus wasn't meant to die!

But Jesus knew that He had <u>come to die</u>! It was all part of **God's plan**. So Jesus told Peter off!

Did you know?

Satan always wants to <u>spoil</u> God's plans. That's why Jesus talks about Satan in v33.

God's plans are <u>always</u> best! Peter will find that out **soon**—and so will we, as we continue reading Mark's book!

PRAY
Thank God that His plans are always best. But sometimes they are hard to understand, so ask God to help you to trust Him, even when you find it hard.

FOLLOWING THE KING

Mark 8v34-35

There are more *tricky terms* in today's reading. Follow the lines to see what they mean.

"Deny himself"

"Take up his cross and follow me"

The gospel

The good news about Jesus.

Means not living to please ourselves, but to please Jesus.

Being prepared to suffer (being made fun of, maybe even dying) out of love for Jesus.

Jesus is the **King**.
Following Him is the *best* thing you can do.
But it <u>won't</u> be easy...

READ
Mark 8v34-35

Yesterday, we saw that Jesus would **suffer**, be **rejected** and **die**! Following Jesus means <u>sharing</u> His suffering, and His rejection, and maybe even dying for Him!

Did You know?

In some countries it can be dangerous to be a Christian. Followers of Jesus may be attacked, kicked out of their jobs or homes, or even killed! **Pray** for people who suffer like this for being Christians. Ask God to help them to be brave, and to keep following Him, even when that's dangerous.

What about you and me?

If we follow Jesus as our King, that means putting Him <u>first</u> in our lives.

E.g. Telling a friend that you can't go skating with her because it's at the same time as your weekly group at church; or switching off the TV to make time to pray; or not joining in with gossip, even if you get laughed at.

If you can, talk to an older Christian about putting Jesus first.

PRAY

Ask Jesus to help you to keep following Him, even if that means suffering in some way. And remember that following Jesus as your King is <u>always</u> the **best** way to live!

WHAT A CHANGE!

Mark 9v2-8

Use the *Change Chart*, to *change* each letter for the letter <u>opposite</u> it. *E.g. A become N, P becomes C.*

G E N A F S V T H E N G V B A

T _ _ _ _ _ _ _ _ _ _ _ _ _ _

Huh? I've *changed* the word—but I still don't know what it means!

Transfiguration means to **change** what someone or something looks like. In today's story there's a HUGE **change** in what Jesus looks like...

READ
Mark 9v2-8

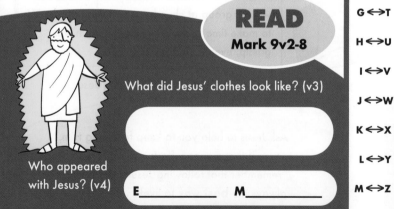

What did Jesus' clothes look like? (v3)

Who appeared with Jesus? (v4)

E_____   M_____

Change Chart

A ⟷ N
B ⟷ O
C ⟷ P
D ⟷ Q
E ⟷ R
F ⟷ S
G ⟷ T
H ⟷ U
I ⟷ V
J ⟷ W
K ⟷ X
L ⟷ Y
M ⟷ Z

Elijah and Moses served God in the Old Testament. But now they were here with Jesus! Peter wanted to make shelters for them all —but he needed to realise that **Jesus** is <u>far greater</u> than Moses or Elijah.

Then God spoke from a cloud. What did He say about Jesus? (v7)

This is my **S**_____, whom I love. **L**_____ to Him!

Six days earlier, Jesus told His disciples He was going to die. They didn't want to believe Him. But what does God tell them to do? (v7)

L_____ to Jesus.

PRAY

Jesus is going to tell His followers <u>why</u> He has come, and what sort of King He will be. They need to **listen** carefully, and believe what He tells them. Ask God to help <u>you</u> to listen to Jesus too (as you read His words in Mark's book), and to believe what He says.

The disciples have learned some <u>amazing</u> things about Jesus. *Use yesterday's Change Chart to find out what they are.*

- Jesus is the **X V A T**   K _ _ _   (Day 1)
- Jesus came to **Q V R**   _ _ _   (Day 2)
- Jesus is **T B Q'F F B A**   _ _ _ _ '_ _ _ _   (Day 4)

The disciples have a <u>lot</u> to tell people! But not yet...

READ
Mark 9v9-10

When can they tell everyone? (v9)
- a) Now
- b) Never
- c) After Jesus (the Son of Man) had risen from the dead.

But <u>first</u>, they have to

Y V F G R A   _ _ _ _ _ _

to Jesus—as God told them yesterday.

READ
Mark 9v11-13

In the Old Testament, God promised that a prophet like Elijah would come <u>just before</u> God's promised King. *Use the Change Chart to see who he was.*

W B U A   G U R   O N C G V F G
J
_ _ _ _ → _ _ _

We know this was John because Matthew explains it in his book—in Matthew 17v10-13.

John had told people to get ready for the promised King. But John also suffered and was killed. The same would happen to Jesus—He would suffer and be killed (v12).

THINK + PRAY

Jesus is God's Son, the King—but He came to die! The disciples don't understand *why* yet—but <u>we</u> can have a sneak preview! **Jesus came to**

E R F P H R   H F   _ _ _ _ _ _ _   _ _

(*We'll find out more about how Jesus rescues us on Day 13.*) *Thank God for sending Jesus as our Rescuing King.*

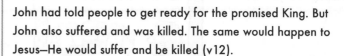

MISSION IMPOSSIBLE?

Peter, James and John had been on a mountain with Jesus.

When they came down, they saw the rest of the disciples.

They had been arguing with the religious leaders about a man and his son.

The boy had an evil spirit in him. It was making him ill.

The man had asked the disciples to heal his son...

...but they couldn't!

So, when Jesus arrived, the man asked Him for help.

Help us—if you can.

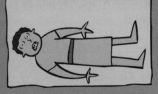

Taken from Mark 9v14-22.

What did Jesus say to the man? (v23)

READ
Mark 9v23-27

Everything is

Did you know?

All things are possible for us when we believe, because all things are possible for *the one we believe in—Jesus!*

When Jesus told the evil spirit to leave the boy, it did! It <u>had</u> to obey Jesus!

How much faith do you think the father had? (v24)

None / A little / Lots and lots

It's not about **how much** faith we have (*phew!*), but **who** we put our faith in.

PRAY — Thank God that **anything** is possible if we believe in Him!

DAY 7 PRAY DAY

Flashback

Back in **Mark** 6, Jesus sent His disciples to the local villages. They **drove** out evil spirits, and healed sick people. But it wasn't by their <u>own</u> **power**! Jesus had **given** them the authority to do it. (Mark 6v7)

That's odd! In yesterday's **story** they <u>couldn't</u> drive out the evil **spirit**! Why not?

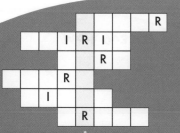

Good question! *Fit the red words into the puzzle to find out.*

What did Jesus tell His disciples? (v29)

> This kind can only come out by **p**_____.

THINK SPOT

- Maybe the disciples had forgotten that it was *Jesus'* power that drove out evil spirits—not their own.
- Or maybe they still *refused to believe* that Jesus had come to <u>die</u>. (*He tells them again in v31, but they still don't understand it.*)

Whatever the problem was, it had <u>stopped</u> them from praying.

READ Mark 9v28-32

P_____

THINK + PRAY

Is there anything <u>you</u> are worried about? Or that you're struggling to do? Spend some time now *praying* about it. Ask God to help you. And remember what we learned yesterday—**anything** is possible if we believe in God!

READ

Mark 9v33-37

Welcome to Jesus' topsy turvy teaching about being first (or is that **last**???).

No, this isn't a printing mistake!

What had the disciples been arguing about? (v34)

Who's the g_____

What did Jesus say to them? (v35)

If anyone wants to be f_____, he must be the very l_____, and the s_____ of all.

What else did Jesus say? (v37)

Whoever w_____ one of these c_____ in my name welcomes m_____.

In those days, children weren't seen as important. They were nobodies! But **Jesus** loved them—and told His followers to welcome them too.

So, who are the **greatest** in Jesus' kingdom? Tick your answers.

Those who...
- [ ] think they're important
- [ ] help others
- [ ] are humble (not proud)
- [ ] push themselves forward

THINK + PRAY

- Wow! That's topsy turvy teaching!
- The way to be the **greatest** is to be a **servant**!
- Welcoming **children** (and serving them) is a way of welcoming **Jesus!**

Jesus also said that whenever we **serve** someone else, we are really **serving Jesus!** How can **you** be a servant this week?

- [ ] Clean your room (without being asked!)
- [ ] Offer to wash up for a week
- [ ] Make a cake or a card for someone who's ill.
- [ ] Clean the car (inside as well!)
- [ ] _____ ← Add one of your own.

Tick two—then ask God to help you to do them!

DAY 9 COMING TO JESUS

What's the best present you've ever been given? *Draw it here.*

Did you pay anything for it?   Yes / No

We're skipping ahead a little bit in Mark to read about the **best present** in the world. And it's FREE!

READ
Mark 10v13-16

The disciples tried to <u>stop</u> the people from bringing children to Jesus. How did Jesus feel about that? (v14)

Children matter to Jesus. <u>Everyone</u> matters to Him!

PRAY
Stop for a moment to **thank Jesus** that <u>you</u> matter to Him.

Present Code

 = A

 = E

 = F

 = G

 = I

 = R

 = S

 = T

Jesus wants <u>everyone</u> to be His friends, and to follow Him as King of their lives. (*That's what "receiving the kingdom of God" means in v15.*)

Do you have to **pay** to enter God's kingdom? Crack the present code to find the answer.

_ _ _   _ _ , _ _ _ _ _   _ _ _ _

Wow! You <u>don't</u> have to pay anything! You <u>can't</u> earn it by being good. It's a free gift!

Do you know any little children? What do they do when someone offers them a present? Do they try to pay for it? Of course not!!! They just take it!

Jesus said that belonging to His kingdom is like a little child getting a present (v15). It's a free gift. We'll find out more about that on Day 13. **Thank Jesus** that belonging to His kingdom is a free gift.

PRAY

DAY 10 TREASURE SEEKER

xtb Mark 10v17-23

Yesterday, we saw that belonging to God's kingdom is a *free gift*.
But today, we meet someone who thinks he can **do** something to earn it. He had a question for Jesus:

What must I do to receive eternal life?

This man already kept God's laws. (*We can read about that in v17-20.*) He seemed to live a good life. But Jesus knew there was something the man loved _more_ than God...

READ
Mark 10v21-23

What did Jesus tell the man? (v21)

poor *follow* *treasure* *sell*

S_____ everything you have and give to the p_____, and you will have t_____ in heaven. Then come, f_____ me.

Circle the correct answers. (v22)

The man went away **happy/sick/sad** because he had great **camels/wealth/riches**.

This man was <u>very</u> rich. When it came to the crunch, his **money** meant more to him than eternal life with **Jesus**!

The man went away feeling sad. I think Jesus was probably sad too.

THINK + PRAY

The man had to decide what was <u>most important</u> to him. Was **Jesus** and His kingdom going to be number one? Or his **money**? Sadly, he decided that his money and possessions were more important than eternal life.

We <u>all</u> need to decide whether following Jesus is more important to us than anything else. (*E.g. more important than money, great clothes, computer games, friends, being on a sports team...*) Do **you** want Jesus to be number one in your life? (It may mean giving something else up!) Think about it, then talk to God about your answer.

DAY 11 GOT THE HUMP?

 xtb — Mark 10v23-31

Yesterday, we read the sad story about the rich man who chose <u>money</u> instead of <u>eternal life</u>.

Now for a simple question: Which is **easiest**?

For this man (with loads of money) to get to heaven?

Or for this hefty hump-backed camel to squeeze through the tiny hole in a needle?

Now let's see what Jesus says...

READ
Mark 10v23-27

The disciples were bowled over! What did they ask? (v26)

> Who, then, can be
> s_____?

What did Jesus reply? (v27)

> All things are
> p_____ with God.

But Peter had something else on his mind as well.

Again, let's see what Jesus says...

> We have left everything to follow you!

READ
Mark 10v28-31

Jesus promises that His followers will get *loads* more than they've given up!—both <u>now</u> and in <u>heaven</u> (v30).

He also warns that there will be *tough times* (*persecutions*). Sometimes friends or family turn against people who follow Jesus. Sometimes it means giving things up (so that Jesus really is number one).

PRAY

Sounds too hard? Copy the red letters (in order) to remind yourself of Jesus' words.

A___ ___ ___ ___ ___ ___ ___ ___ ___ ___ ___ ___ ___ ___ ___ ___ ___ ___ ___

It is **God** who saves us. And **God** will help us to put Jesus first. *Thank God* for this. Talk to Him about any tough times you're having.

DAY 12 FIRST SERVE

Do you remember the argument the disciples had in Chapter Nine? (Day 8) What were they asking?

> Who's the g_____?

Since then, Jesus has taught them loads of things:

- the way to be *great* is to *serve*;
- belonging to God's kingdom is a *free gift*;
- following Jesus needs to be *more* important to us than anything else;
- *all things* are possible with God.

And He's just told them again that He is going to **die**. (*That's in v32-34.*)

But James and John are still thinking about **greatness**. Their own!!

READ
Mark 10v35-44

J&J (James and John) know that Jesus is God's chosen **King** (the Christ).

Maybe they're imagining Him on a throne...

Where do J&J want to sit? (v37)

On Jesus' _____ and _____

> J&J want to be GREAT!
> But God's kingdom is different.
> God's kingdom is **upside down!**

If you want to be f_____, you've got to be l_____. And the way to be g_____ is to s_____!

serve   great   last   first

Did You Know?

When Jesus talks about "drinking the cup" and "being baptised" like Him (v38), He's talking about His death! It's the cup full of God's anger that He "drank" for us when He died on the cross. Do you think J&J wanted that type of greatness??!!

Time to serve

Check back to the list on Day 8. Have you done the things you ticked yet? Well done if you have!
Now tick <u>another</u> one!—and write down here the day you will do it.

PRAY
Ask God to help you do it!

SECOND SERVE

Jesus has just told His followers that <u>they</u> need to be **servants**. Now let's see what He says about <u>Himself</u>.

READ
Mark 10v45

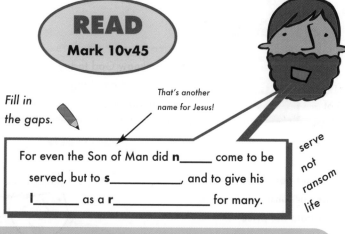

That's another name for Jesus!

Fill in the gaps.

> For even the Son of Man did **n_____** come to be served, but to **s_____**, and to give his **l_____** as a **r_____** for many.

serve
not
ransom
life

Wow! Jesus is the **King**—but He came to **serve!** He's the *Servant King.*

Why? Take the <u>first</u> letter of each picture to find out.

Jesus came to __ __ __ __ __ the problem of __ __ __

Did you know?

Sin is more than just doing wrong things. Sin is doing what **we** want instead of what **God** wants. Sin is a HUGE problem—because it <u>separates</u> us from God.

The great news is that Jesus came to <u>solve</u> the problem of sin. *Read The Servant King on the next page to find out more.*

Time to Think
- Are **you** a follower of Jesus?
- Do you want to be? (*Go back to The Servant King if you're not sure.*)

PRAY

Thank Jesus that He came as our Servant King, to "give His life as a ransom for many"—including you!

THE SERVANT KING

How does Jesus solve the problem of sin? It's explained in Mark 10v45, where Jesus says that He...

> **...did not come to be served, but to serve, and to give his life as a ransom for many.**
> (*Mark 10v45*)

Jesus is the **Christ**—God's Chosen King. And He's the **Son of God**. He's awesome! He's in charge of everything. *BUT* He came as a <u>servant</u>! To help and save us. He loves us so much that He came to <u>rescue</u> us from our sin.

Why do we need rescuing?
Sin gets in the way between us and God. It stops us from knowing Him and stops us being His friends. The final result of sin is death. You can see why we need rescuing!

How did Jesus rescue us?
At the first Easter, when Jesus was about 33 years old, He was crucified. He was nailed to a cross and left to die.

As He died, all the sins of the world (all the wrongs people do) were put onto Jesus. He took all of our sin onto Himself, taking the punishment we deserve.

A *ransom* is money paid to set people free. Jesus died in our place, as our ransom—buying our freedom. <u>Jesus</u> paid the price for <u>our</u> sins.

When Jesus died, He dealt with the problem of sin. That means there is <u>nothing</u> to separate us from God any more. That's great news for you and me!

> We can know God today as our Friend and King—and one day live in heaven with Him forever.

Did you know?
Jesus died on the cross as our Rescuer—but He didn't stay dead! After three days, God brought Him back to life! Jesus is still alive today, ruling as our King.

Have YOU been rescued by Jesus? Turn to the next page to find out more...

AM I A CHRISTIAN?

Not sure if you're a Christian? Then check it out below...

> **Christians are people who have been rescued by Jesus and follow Him as King.**

> **You can't become a Christian by trying to be good.**

That's great news, since you can't be totally good all the time!

It's about accepting what Jesus did on the cross to rescue you. To do that, you will need to **ABCD**.

A **Admit** your sin—that you do, say and think wrong things. Tell God you are sorry. Ask Him to forgive you, and to help you to change. There will be some wrong things you have to stop doing.

B **Believe** that Jesus died for you, to take the punishment for your sin; that He came back to life, and that He is still alive today.

C **Consider** the cost of living like God's friend from now on, with Him in charge. It won't be easy. Ask God to help you do this.

D **Do** something about it! In the past you've gone your own way rather than God's way. Will you hand control of your life over to Him from now on? If you're ready to ABCD, then talk to God now. The prayer will help you.

A prayer

Dear God,
I have done and said and thought things that are wrong.
I am really sorry.
Please forgive me. Thank you for sending Jesus to die for me.
From now on, please help me to live as one of Your friends, with You in charge.
Amen

> **Jesus welcomes <u>everyone</u> who comes to Him. If you have put your trust in Him, He has rescued you from your sins and will help you to live for Him. That's great news!**

Sign your name here _____

My name is

Alison

But I'm <u>not</u> the **son** of a man called **Ali**!

Today's story is about *Bartimaeus*

He <u>is</u> the **son** of a man called **Timaeus**!

Bartimaeus had a problem. He was <u>blind</u>.

READ
Mark 10v46-52

Jesus and His disciples travelled through **Jericho** on their way to **Jerusalem**.

(Circle) Jericho on the map.

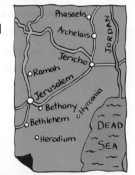

Bartimaeus shouted loudly to Jesus. (v47)

Jesus, **S_____** of **D_____**, have mercy on me!

mercy means undeserved kindness

Son of David is another name for the *Christ*, God's chosen King. Bartimaeus <u>believed</u> that Jesus was the King.

What did Bartimaeus want? (v51)

To _____

What did Jesus tell him? (v52)

Your **f_____** has healed you.

faith means trust

When was Bartimaeus healed? (v52)

Never / Next week / At once

Then Bartimaeus *followed* Jesus.

B D E F I L O V W

Bartimaeus __ __ __ __ __ __ __ in Jesus.

Bartimaeus __ __ __ __ __ __ __ __ Jesus.

THINK + PRAY

Do **you** <u>believe</u> in Jesus and <u>follow</u> Him?
- *If you do, it's because <u>God</u> has given you the faith to do so. Thank God for giving you that faith.*
- *If you're not sure, <u>ask God</u> to help you to believe, and to learn more about Jesus as you read the Bible.*

DAY 15   # THE KING IS HERE

Unjumble the **blue** words (*they're backwards!*) to see what was written in the <u>Old Testament</u> about the **Christ** (God's chosen King).

Shout for yoj _____*, you people of Jerusalem.*

Look, your gniK _____ *is coming to you!*

He comes triumphant and victorious,

but humble and riding on a yeknod _____

—on a tloc _____, *the foal of a donkey.* (Zechariah 9v9)

Find out how these words came true in today's story.

READ
Mark 11v1-11

Jesus and His disciples had travelled from Jericho. *Draw a line from Jericho to Jerusalem on yesterday's map.*

When people saw Jesus riding into Jerusalem on a donkey, they got really excited! What were they shouting? (v9)

> God bless him who
> **c**_____ in the
> name of the **L**_____!

500 years earlier, Zechariah had said that God's chosen **King**, who had come to **rescue** His people, would ride into Jerusalem on a <u>colt</u> (a young donkey). No wonder the people got excited! *Take the first letter of each picture to see what else they shouted.*

_ _ _ _ _ _ _ _

Hosanna means "Lord, save us". They were <u>right</u> that Jesus was their **King**, who had come to **save** them. But they didn't understand <u>how</u> He would save them...

Did you know?

Your Bible may call this story "The Triumphal Entry"—because Jesus entered Jerusalem in triumph (victory). **BUT**, just a few days later, these crowds would shout to have Jesus killed!

PRAY

Jesus rode into Jerusalem on a **donkey**—just as God had said. He came to **save** His people—just as God had promised. Thank God that His words <u>always</u> come true.

TABLE TURNING

Spot the Difference. *There are ten to find.*

Read the verses to find out what's happening.

READ
Mark 11v12-19

Circle the ten mistakes in the story.

On the way in to Manchester, Jesus saw an oak tree. But when He reached it, there were no apples on it. When Jesus reached the Temple, He began to drive out those who were dancing there. He overturned the wheelbarrows of the money-changers, and the bicycles of those selling parrots. He said, "It is written, 'My house will be called a palace of prayer for all nations—but you have made it an igloo of robbers.'" Then the religious leaders began to look for a way to thank Jesus.

Answers: Manchester, oak, apples, dancing, wheelbarrows, bicycles, parrots, palace, igloo, thank.

What had God said His Temple should be called? (v17)

A **H**_____ of **P**_____

BUT—the Temple courtyard was full of lying salesmen. The people who came to pray were *cheated* out of their money! So Jesus stopped the salesmen.

THINK + PRAY

Sometimes we see things happening that we know are wrong. *E.g. if you see someone take money from the teacher's desk, or if nobody will talk to a new boy at school.* If you see something like that, ask God to help you to act in the way He wants you to, even when that's difficult or could make you unpopular.

DAY 17 — FIGGY FAIRH

Yesterday, Jesus went to look at a fig tree—but it had no figs! Jesus said that no one would ever eat figs from it again.
In today's story, that same tree is dead...

READ
Mark 11v20-25

These verses are tricky to understand. *But crack the arrow code to see what the BIG idea is.*

— — — —   — — —   — — — — — —

(v22)

On Day 6, we found out about <u>faith</u> (trust). We discovered that, "it's not about **how much** faith we have, but **who** we put our faith in."

PRAY **God** is wonderful, powerful and loving. <u>Nothing</u> is impossible for Him! Thank God for this.

Arrow Code

⇧ = A
↘ = D
⇩ = E
↗ = F
⇐ = G
↘ = H
↑ = I
↗ = J
↙ = N
← = O
▷ = S
◁ = T
▽ = U
▷ = V

Did you know?

In case you're wondering about that fig tree...
The fig tree was like a *picture* of the Temple. The fig tree <u>looked</u> good from a distance—but had no figs. The Temple looked good too—but was actually full of lying salesmen!

READ   verse 23 again

Does that mean we can ask for <u>anything</u> at all—and as long as we believe, we'll get it?!

No, 'fraid not! God isn't promising to give us <u>everything</u> we want. Or to solve all our problems straight away. And He definitely <u>won't</u> give us anything wrong or sinful! **BUT** when we ask, with faith, for things that are right, God *can* and *will* give them to us.

PRAY You can pray about anything! Ask God to help you to **trust Him** to give good, loving answers.

It's time for tricky questions (and tricky stuff to understand!). Hold onto your hats as we whizz through it...

Tricky Temple Turnout
Jesus had toppled tables and turfed out the lying salesmen who were cheating people in the Temple. Because of this, the religious leaders were looking for a way to **kill** Jesus!

Tricky Question Number One
The religious leaders came to Jesus with a trick question. But they didn't want to know the answer! They just wanted to get Jesus into trouble...

READ
Mark 11v27-28

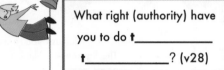

What right (authority) have you to do t_____ t_____? (v28)

In other words, "What gives **you** the right to kick people out of the Temple?"

But they were just trying to <u>trap</u> Jesus—so He asked them a tricky question of His own...

READ
Mark 11v29-33

Tricky Question Number Two
Who was Jesus' question about? (v30)

J_____ the Baptist

John the Baptist had told people to get ready for **Jesus**, God's promised King.

So the question was—did John's message about Jesus come from **God** or not?

How did the religious leaders answer? (v33)

We

- If they said John's message came from **God**, it would be like saying that <u>Jesus</u> came from God too!
- But if they said it <u>wasn't</u> from God, the crowds might turn against them. (v32)

So they said they didn't know!

PRAY

The religious leaders were stumped by Jesus' tricky question! **BUT** if <u>you</u> come to Jesus with a true question, really wanting to know more about Him, then He will always show you the answer. What would you like to ask Jesus? Talk to Him about it now.

What's the difference between a parrot, a parable and a parachute?

Jesus only used <u>one</u> of them to teach us stuff!

Here is Jesus' parable from Mark 12:

A man planted a vineyard, with a wall and a watchtower.

Then he rented the vineyard to tenants, and went on a journey.

At harvest time, the man sent a servant to collect some fruit from the vineyard.

But the tenants beat the servant, and sent him back with nothing.

The owner sent more servants, but each one was beaten or killed.

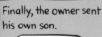
Finally, the owner sent his own son.

They will respect my son.

But the tenants decided to kill the son.

Let's kill him!

Then the vineyard will be ours.

So they killed the son, and threw his body out of the vineyard.

READ
Mark 12v1-8

This parable uses picture language. It works like this:
The owner of the vineyard = **God**.
The vineyard = the **Israelites** (Jews).
The tenants = the Jewish **religious leaders**.
The servants = **God's messengers** (prophets).

The final character in the story is the owner's son. Who do you think he is? (*Think carefully, then use the code from Day 17 to check your answer.*)

↗ ⇓ ▷ ▽ ▷

_ _ _ _ _

PRAY

Mark's book shows us again and again that **Jesus** is God's Son. He is the promised King, sent to rescue us. *Thank God for keeping His promise to send Jesus.*

By the way: As the parable shows, the religious leaders had rejected God's messengers (including John the Baptist), and now they were looking for a way to <u>kill</u> Jesus. But it all turns out to be part of <u>God's plan</u>—as we'll see tomorrow...

A BIG MISTAKE?

Re-read yesterday's cartoon story.

How would you feel if you were the owner of the vineyard?

READ
Mark 12v9

Those wicked tenants thought they would get away with it—but they'd made a **BIG MISTAKE!**

What will the owner do? (v9)

• The tenants would be

_____

• The vineyard will be given to

_____

This parable is about the religious leaders. They <u>don't believe</u> that Jesus is God's promised King. So they've decided to **kill** Him! But they've made a **BIG MISTAKE** about Jesus...

READ
Mark 12v10-12

In most Bible versions, v10 talks about a **capstone** (or *cornerstone*).

No—it's not a stone wearing a cap! The **capstone** is the <u>most important</u> stone in a building.

The religious leaders had made a BIG MISTAKE about Jesus. He was the <u>most important</u> person they would ever meet. He was *God's chosen King*, sent to <u>rescue</u> His people.

A BIG MISTAKE?
The religious leaders succeeded with their wicked plot. They <u>did</u> have Jesus killed. (*That's in the last part of Mark's book.*)

But it <u>wasn't</u> a mistake!!!
Jesus had already told His followers that He had <u>come</u> to die.
It was all part of **God's plan**.

Copy all the red letters to see why Jesus died.

— — — — — — — — —

If you're not sure <u>how</u> Jesus rescues us, then turn back to *The Servant King* after Day 13.

PRAY Thank God for sending His Son Jesus to be your Rescuer.

DAY 21 HEROES AND ZEROS

Welcome to the book of **Judges**. It's chock full of *heroes*!
But there are some *zeros* as well! (*As we'll see...*)

Judges follows straight on from the book of **Joshua**.
So let's set the scene by looking back at a verse from Joshua:

> *Take the first letter of each picture.*

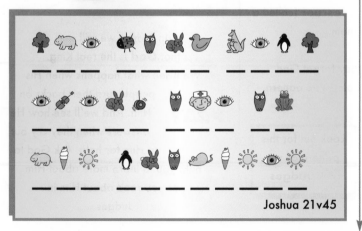

Joshua 21v45

Wow!
God had kept <u>every one</u> of His promises to the Israelites! He had brought them safely into the land of Canaan. Surely the Israelites will **trust** God and **obey** Him from now on?

To find out, we're going to flick to the very <u>last</u> verse in Judges.

READ
Judges 21v25

Fill in the gaps.

> In those days Israel has no **k**_____;
> **e**_____ did just as he pleased.

Instead of obeying **God** and doing what <u>He</u> said—they just did what <u>they</u> wanted!

Turn over to the next page to find out more.

DAY 21
CONTINUED

ROUND AND ROUND

 Judges 21v25

There's a sad pattern in the book of **Judges**. The same story circles round again and again. It looks like this:

God's people disobeyed Him.

God sent a rescuer to save His people.

God allowed their enemies to defeat them.

God's people called out to Him, saying, "Save us!"

The time of the Judges lasted for **400 years**. During that time, the Israelites kept <u>forgetting</u> what God had done for them...

- They **disobeyed** God.
- God allowed their enemies to **defeat** them.
- Then the Israelites **cried out** to God to rescue them.
- God sent them a **rescuer** (called a Judge) to save them.

GREAT! But then they forgot God again, and the whole circle pattern started up again...

Look out for this pattern as we read **Judges**.

By the way—the last verse in Judges says that they didn't have a king. It's true that they didn't have a <u>man</u> as king. But they **did** have a King! Who was their King?

__ __ __

PRAY

In Judges we will see that **God** is the real King. We'll see what happens when His people turn their backs on Him. And we'll see how He answers when they cry out to Him for help. Ask God to help <u>you</u> to learn more about Him as you read about Him in Judges.

DAY 22 **A GOOD START**

xtb — Judges 1v1-4

Spot the Difference. There are *six* to find.

Jon and Sarah both ask what their Gran wants them to do. But there's a *difference*:

—**Jon** has already decided to help, no matter what his Gran wants him to do.

—**Sarah** is secretly thinking, "If I don't want to do it, I'll tell Gran I'm too busy!"

READ
Judges 1v1-4

What did the people ask? (v1)

> Which of our tribes will be the f_____ to go and attack the Canaanites?

What did God tell them? (v2)

> The tribe of J_____ will go first. I have given the l_____ to them.

The tribe of Judah won their battle. Who gave them victory? (v4)

The Israelites had made a **good start**:

- They *asked God* what to do.
- They *obeyed God*.
- And God kept His *promise* to give them the victory.

But sadly, they'll soon start to mess things up...

THINK + PRAY

The Israelites had asked God what to do, so *that* they could do it. (*They were like <u>Jon</u>, not Sarah.*) What are **you** like when you read your Bible? Are you looking out for God's commands, so *that* you can <u>obey</u> Him? Or do you want to find out what they are first, so that you can <u>choose</u> whether to obey them or not? (*Like Sarah in the puzzle.*) **Talk to God** about your answers. And remember that God will <u>always</u> help you to obey Him, if you ask Him to.

Judges
1v21-30

The Israelites were now living in **Canaan**—the land God promised them. But, <u>before</u> they reached Canaan, God had told them what to do when they were there.

Use the Flag Code to see what God had said.

You must _ _ _ _ _   _ _ _

the people living in the land, and

_ _ _ _ _ _ _ _ _ their idols.

Numbers 33v52

The people living in Canaan <u>didn't</u> believe in God. Instead they prayed to statues (idols). God told the Israelites that they must drive these people out of Canaan. If they didn't, these people would be a problem in the future. They would lead the Israelites to pray to statues too!

<u>Yesterday</u>, we saw that the tribe of Judah got off to a good start. They *asked God* what to do, and *obeyed* Him. But <u>today</u>, there's a sad problem...

Flag Code

◀ = B

▬ = D

▬ = E

● = I

◣ = O

✚ = R

▭ = S

▮ = T

▣ = U

✕ = V

▨ = Y

READ
Judges 1v21

READ
Judges 1v29-30

Did the tribe of Benjamin *drive out* the Jebusites?

Yes / No

Did the tribe of Ephraim *drive out* the Canaanites?

Yes / No

Did the tribe of Zebulun *drive out* the Canaanites?

Yes / No

There are lists like this all through Chapter One. The Israelites did **not** drive out the people of Canaan.

They _ _ _ _ _ _ _ _ _ _ God.

PRAY

The Israelites started well, but then disobeyed God. Are <u>you</u> like that? Do you start well, but then let God down? If so, tell Him you're **sorry**, and ask Him to help you to **change**.

DAY 24 WEEPERS CREEPERS

I promise to help with your maths homework.

And I promise I'll stop taking stuff from your room.

Ever made an agreement?

God made agreements with the Israelites. They're called **covenants**.

God promised to help the Israelites drive out their enemies. The Israelites promised to destroy their enemies' idols (statues), and not to make any agreements with God's enemies.

(You can read about this in Exodus 23v31-33.)

BUT...
Yesterday we saw that the Israelites *disobeyed* God. They did not drive their enemies out. Instead, they made agreements to let them stay in Canaan!

READ
Judges 2v1-5

God told the Israelites:

- I brought you out of **Egypt**
- I led you to the **promised** land
- I promised never to break my **covenant** with you
- I told you **not** to make a covenant with the people of Canaan
- I told you to destroy their **altars**.

(Altars were stone tables where people gave gifts to their gods.)

Fit the blue words into the puzzle.

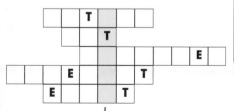

The Israelites had not driven out their enemies. Now those people and their idols (pretend gods) would become a *trap* for the Israelites.

When the Israelites heard this, what did they do? (v4)

What did they call that place? (v5)

B_____ (That means "weepers".)

THINK + PRAY

How do you feel when you realise that you've let God down? Are you upset? Do you talk to Him about it? Do you ask Him to help you to change? Talk to God about it now.

FOLLOW THE LEADER

Flashback

Joshua had been leader of the Israelites ever since Moses died. Joshua was a <u>good</u> leader. He trusted God and obeyed Him.

 READ

Judges 2v6-9

Cross out the X's.

- Joshua **XRXEXMXIXNXDXEXDX** the people of the great things God had done for them.
- Joshua **XEXNXCXOXUXRXAXGXEXDX** the people to trust God and obey Him.

 THINK SPOT

Do you know anyone like Joshua? Someone who reminds you of the great things God has done for you, and helps you to trust and obey God?

Write their name here.

PRAY **Thank God** for this person. (*And find a way to say Thank You to <u>them</u> too!*)

But things changed after Joshua died...

READ

Judges 2v10-11

(Circle) the correct words.

The people **remembered / forgot / ignored** what God had done for them. They did **evil / good / handstands**, and served the **Baals / Balls / Balloons** instead of the one, true God.

PRAY

The Israelites served pretend gods (called Baals) instead of the **one, true God**. Ask God to help you <u>not</u> to be like the Israelites. Ask Him to help you always to **remember** what He has done for you, and to **keep** trusting and obeying Him.

CIRCLE LINE

 Judges 2v12-17

Start here!

After Joshua died, the people forgot about God...

READ
Judges 2v12-13

The Israelites turned _ _ _ _ _ _ _ _ from God. They served pretend gods (like Baal) instead.

READ
Judges 2v14-15

God was _ _ _ _ _ _ with the Israelites. He handed them over to their enemies.

PRAY

This is such a <u>sad</u> pattern. When I read it, I want to shake the Israelites and tell them not to be so silly! God has done so *much* for them. It's silly to turn away from Him!
God has done so *much* for you and me, too! Ask God to help you <u>not</u> to turn away from Him.

Look back at the pattern on the second page of **Day 21** to see how this same story circles round again and again.

READ
Judges 2v16

God provided a _ _ _ _ _ _ to rescue His people.

The Israelites turned _ _ _ _ from God—again!

READ
Judges 2v17

xtb Judges 2v18-19

The wonderful truth about God.

Take the first letter of each picture.

- God shows us _ _ _ _ _

- God shows us _ _ _ _ _

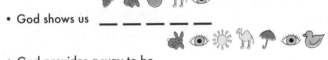
- God provides a way to be _ _ _ _ _ _

> **Did you know?**
>
> **Grace** is God's HUGE kindness to people who <u>don't</u> deserve it. **Mercy** is God decision to help us and <u>not</u> treat us the way we deserve.

The sad truth about people.

- We all _ _ _

> **Did you know?**
>
> **Sin** is doing what <u>we</u> want instead of what <u>God</u> wants.

READ
Judges 2v18-19

- Which verse shows us that God rescues His people because of His <u>mercy</u> and <u>grace</u>? Verse _____

- Which verse shows us that people all <u>sin</u>? Verse _____

These things are just as true today. We <u>all</u> sin. We <u>all</u> need to be rescued. And God has shown His *mercy* and *grace* by sending us a Rescuer.

Who did God send as our Rescuer? _ _ _ _ _

Turn to *The Servant King* after Day 13 to remind yourself how Jesus rescues us from sin.

PRAY Thank God for His mercy and grace to you. Thank Him for sending Jesus as your Rescuer.

JUDGE NUMBER ONE

 Judges 3v7-11

We've seen the circle pattern in the book of Judges. Now it's time to meet the first Judge...

READ
Judges 3v7-11

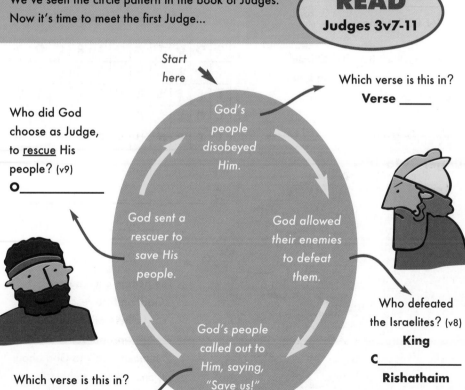

Start here

God's people disobeyed Him.

Which verse is this in?
Verse _____

Who did God choose as Judge, to rescue His people? (v9)

O_____

God sent a rescuer to save His people.

God allowed their enemies to defeat them.

God's people called out to Him, saying, "Save us!"

Which verse is this in?
Verse _____

Who defeated the Israelites? (v8)
King
C_____
Rishathaim

What was Othniel given? (v10)

The S_____ of the L_____

This means that **God** had <u>chosen</u> Othniel, and would give him the power to rescue the Israelites.

Did you know?

Othniel's uncle was called *Caleb* (v9). He was one of the 12 spies sent by Moses to check out the promised land. You can read about Caleb—and how he <u>trusted</u> God—in Numbers 13v25–14v9.

PRAY

When the people cried out for help, God sent them a *rescuer* (Othniel). God has sent <u>us</u> a Rescuer, too—His Son, Jesus. **Thank God** for sending Jesus as your Rescuer.

Are you right- or left-handed? _____

Today's story is about a left-handed Judge, and a V-E-R-Y fat king...

As we saw yesterday, God sent <u>Othniel</u> to rescue the Israelites. But after Othniel died, the people *turned away* from God again. God was angry, and let fat King Eglon defeat the Israelites. The people cried out to God, and He sent them a left-handed Judge to rescue them...

READ
Judges 3v15-18

Ehud hid a **sword** under his clothes. It was strapped to his **right** thigh, because he was left-handed.

Ehud said he had a message from **God** for the king. So Eglon sent all his servants away. With his **left** hand, Ehud grabbed his hidden sword and killed the king. Then Ehud left the room, and **locked** the door behind him.

The king's servants thought he was on the **toilet**! Eventually, they unlocked the door and found King Eglon dead.

Meanwhile, Ehud escaped. He called the Israelites with his **trumpet** and led them to victory over Eglon's army. God then gave them **peace** in the land for 80 years.

You can read this story in Judges 3v18-30.

Find all of the **yellow** words in the wordsearch. *Some are backwards!*

G	O	D	T	H	G	I	R	G	O	D
T	O	I	L	E	T	E	C	A	E	P
T	F	E	L	R	E	S	C	U	E	D
L	O	C	K	E	D	D	R	O	W	S
T	E	P	M	U	R	T	T	H	E	M

What do the leftover letters spell?

G _ _ _   _ _ _ _ _ _ _

_ _ _ _

PRAY

The people cried out to God, and He rescued them. Is there anything <u>you</u> are worried about at the moment? Talk to God about it, and ask Him to help. He will!

Yesterday, we met **Ehud**, the left–handed rescuer. Now let's see what happened after Ehud died...

READ
Judges 4v1

What did the people do after Ehud died?

The people had followed God while Ehud was alive. But after he died, they *turned away* from God again!

A *different kind of* **rescue** was needed. One that changed things for <u>ever</u>. And for that, we need a *different kind of* **Rescuer**...

B   D   E   F   L   O   R   S   V

"Jesus _ _ _ _ _ us and has _ _ _ _ _ us from our sins by his _ _ _ _ _ _."

Revelation 1v5

Wow! Jesus <u>loves</u> us! He loves us so much, that He came to die for us.

Jesus has done what Ehud could never do. He has <u>freed</u> us from our sins.

How did Jesus rescue us? By <u>dying</u> for us, so that we can be forgiven, if we trust in Him.

THINK + PRAY

Nothing that **Ehud** did could change the <u>hearts</u> of the Israelites. They were still sinful people, who turned away from God. No *left-handed rescuer* could set them free from sin.

But **Jesus** has *nail-scarred hands* (from the cross). He <u>died</u> to solve the problem of sin, so that we can be forgiven, and live with Him for ever in heaven. Thank Jesus for loving you so much that He died to rescue you.

FULL CIRCLE

 Judges 6v1-10

The circle pattern of Judges carried on:

After Ehud died, the Israelites turned away from God. (Judges 4v1)

God chose Deborah to be their Judge, and rescue them. (Judges 4v4–5v31)

God allowed Jabin, a Canaanite king, to defeat them. (Judges 4v2)

The Israelites cried out to God to save them. (Judges 4v3)

Did You Know?

Deborah was the only Judge who was a woman. You can read her story in Judges 4.

Sadly, the circle pattern <u>still</u> carried on. After Deborah, the Israelites turned away from God again!

READ
Judges 6v1-6

Cross out the <u>wrong</u> words.

The Israelites were defeated by the **Canaanites / Midianites / Stalagmites**, and had to hide in **trees / rivers / caves**. Whenever the Israelites planted crops, their enemies came and **ruined / cooked / watered** their crops.

Then the Israelites cried out to God to save them.

READ
Judges 6v7-10

Fill in the missing words.

listen   land   Egypt   not

I brought you out of **E**_____. (v8)

I gave you this **l**_____. (v9)

I told you **n**_____ to worship the gods of the Amorites. But you did not **l**_____ to me. (v10)

PRAY

God had done *great* things for the Israelites—but they didn't <u>listen</u> to Him or <u>obey</u> Him. Ask God to help **you** to listen to what He says in the Bible, and to obey His words.

DAY 32 — MIGHTY WARRIOR!

The Lord is with you, Mighty Warrior!

Who do you think the angel is speaking to?
—a strong and brave man?
—a powerful soldier?
—a mighty leader?

READ
Judges 6v11-12

The next Judge is called **Gideon**. He isn't strong and brave. In fact, he's so scared of the Midianites that he's working inside a wine tub to keep safe!

But what does the angel tell him? (v12)

Take the first letter of each pic.

_ _ _ _ _   _ _ _ _ _ _ _

READ
Judges 6v13-14

Gideon has loads of questions!

> If God is with us, why is all this happening?

> Why isn't God doing the miracles He did in Egypt?

But what does God tell Gideon? (v14)

_ _ _ _ _ _ _ _ _ _ _

Wow! God **is** going to defeat the Midianites. And He's going to use Gideon to do it!

READ
Judges 6v15-16

Gideon **still** isn't sure! He thinks he's too weak. But what does God say again? (v16)

_ _ _ _ _ _ _

_ _ _ _ _ _ _

Gideon wanted to be sure that it was **God** speaking to Him. So He prepared a gift for God. The angel touched the gift with his staff—and it burst into flames. Then the angel disappeared. Now Gideon knew for sure that the message was from God. (v17-24)

PRAY

Gideon had loads of doubts and questions. But God was patient with Gideon, and promised to be with him. Do **you** have doubts and questions about God? Tell Him! He will help you find the answers.

DAY 33 JERUB-BAAL *

This was a new name for Gideon. It means "Let Baal defend himself." Why was Gideon given such an odd name? Today's story will tell you.

xtb Judges 6v25-32

The Israelites had turned away from God. They prayed to <u>pretend</u> gods—called Baal and Asherah—instead of the **One, True God**!

Gideon's dad had an altar to the pretend god, Baal. (An altar was a stone table where people gave gifts to their gods.) But the <u>real</u> God told Gideon to destroy that altar...

Tear down your father's altar to Baal...

BAAL

...and cut down the Asherah pole beside it.

Then build an altar to the LORD your God instead.

So Gideon took ten servants with him.

They destroyed the altar to Baal.

They built an altar to God instead, and burnt a bull on it as a gift for God.

But they did it at **night**, so that no-one would see them!

READ Judges 6v28-32

This story is in Judges 6v25-27.

When the people found out what Gideon had done, they wanted to kill him! But what did Gideon's dad say? (v31)

defend   Baal   god

If **B**_____ really is a **g**_____, he can **d**_____ himself!

What a great answer from Gideon's dad! If Baal is a <u>real</u> god, he can look after himself. He doesn't need the townsmen to fight for him!

PRAY

One of the great truths we discover in Judges is that **God** is the One, True God. **He** is in charge. <u>Nothing</u> can stop His plans! *Thank* God for being like this.

DAY 34 FLEX THAT FLEECE!

If it's <u>not</u> raining at lunchtime, that means God wants me to go and see John.

But if it <u>is</u> raining, that means God doesn't want me to go.

Hmm... what's that all about???
It's sort-of based on today's story about Gideon...

The Midianites (and some other tribes) came trampling over the land of the Israelites again. Gideon called some men together to fight them. But first, he wanted to be totally sure that God had chosen <u>him</u> to rescue the Israelites...

READ
Judges 6v36-40

 Circle the correct answers.

Day 1 (v36-38)
Gideon put a wool fleece on the ground. He asked God to make the fleece **wet / dry**, and the ground **wet / dry**. When Gideon squeezed out the fleece the next day, there was **no water / a few drops / a bowlful**.

Day 2 (v39-40)
This time, Gideon asked God to make the fleece **wet / dry**, and the ground **wet / dry**. When Gideon squeezed out the fleece the next day, there was **no water / a few drops / a bowlful**.

Wow! God did what Gideon asked. Now Gideon was really sure that God had chosen him.

---

 xtb Judges 6v33-40

THINK SPOT

Sometimes, people think this story means that we can set <u>tests</u> for God, to find out what He wants us to do. In fact, the teenager in the cartoon at the beginning was **me**!!!

But this is a <u>wrong</u> way to treat God! Most of the time, we already <u>know</u> how to live for God because He shows us in the Bible. We don't need to "test" Him.

But God is also **patient** with us, and **kind** to us. When we're finding it <u>hard</u> to obey Him—or we're <u>nervous</u>, like Gideon was—then He kindly helps us.
For example, through a verse in the Bible, or the help of a friend, or...

PRAY
Are **you** nervous about obeying God? Ask Him to help you. He will!

DAY 35 MATHS LESSON

Gideon had called together an army to fight the Midianites.

The diagram shows the size of Gideon's army. Each box stands for **100** soldiers. There are **320** boxes in total, showing Gideon's full army of **32,000 soldiers**.

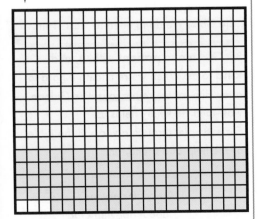

But there's a <u>problem</u> with Gideon's army. *It's too big!*

xtb Judges 7v1-8

READ
Judges 7v1-3

God said that everyone who was <u>scared</u> should go home.

How many men went home? (v3)	a) 12,000
	b) 22,000
	c) 32,000

Shade in 220 boxes on the diagram. (That's all of the <u>yellow</u> boxes.)

Now Gideon only had <u>10,000</u> soldiers left. But his army was *still too big!*

READ
Judges 7v4-8

God told Gideon to keep the men who lapped the water —but to send the rest home.

How many men were left? (v8)	a) 300
	b) 400
	c) 500

That means 9,700 men went home!

Shade in 97 boxes on the diagram. (That's all of the <u>blue</u> boxes.)

Maths Lesson
What's the lesson from all this maths? It's in verse 2. *Read verse 2 again.*

With a BIG army, the Israelites would think that they had saved themselves.

But who was <u>really</u> going to save them?   **G_____**

PRAY

In verse 7, God tells Gideon, "**I will rescue you.**" God is so powerful, that He is <u>always</u> able to save us. Thank Him for being so great.

DAY 36 WHAT A DREAM!

Look again at yesterday's diagram. Gideon had started with a huge army of **32,000** men. But now he only had **300** men left. (The three <u>white</u> boxes on the diagram.)

How do you think Gideon felt?

The enemy army was H-U-G-E! They swarmed across the valley like locusts. Even their camels were too many to count! And Gideon only had 300 men!

But God knew how Gideon was feeling...

READ
Judges 7v9-15

 Draw the man's dream. (v13)

Draw what rolled in to the camp.

Draw what happened to the tent.

The enemy soldiers knew what the dream meant. (v14)

This must be the **s**_____ of

G_____ son of Joash.

G_____ has given him victory over us!

Wow! What a fantastic dream! Gideon <u>praised</u> God. Then he dashed back to tell his men that God was giving them victory over their enemies.

THINK + PRAY

• God knew that **Gideon** was weak and afraid. But God would still use him to rescue the Israelites!

• Never think that **you** are too weak or young or afraid to serve God! If you really mean it, tell God that you want to serve Him with your life.

• When Gideon was afraid, God <u>encouraged</u> him (with the dream). Ask God to encourage you, too.

Follow the maze to find **three promises** God made to Gideon.

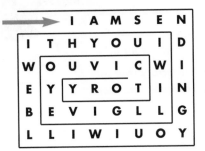

```
I   A M S E N
I T H Y O U I D D
W O U V I C W I N
E Y Y R O T I N G
B E V I G L L L G
L L I W I U O Y
```

_ _ _ _

_ _ _ _ _ _ _ _ _ _ _ _ _

(Judges 6v14)

_ _ _ _ _ _ _ _

_ _ _ _ _ _ _ _ _

(Judges 6v16)

_ _ _ _ _ _ _ _ _ _ _ _ _ _

(Judges 7v7)

READ
Judges 7v16-22

(Circle) the ten mistakes in the story.

Gideon gave each man a trombone, and a jar with a candle inside it. Just before lunchtime, Gideon's men crept to the edge of the enemy caravan site. They blew their clarinets, and broke the plates they were holding. Then they whispered, "A sword for the LORD and for Gladys!" The enemy army attacked each other with their feathers. And then they all swam away.

Answers: trombone, candle, lunchtime, caravan, clarinets, plates, whispered, Gladys, feathers, swam.

Gideon's men didn't have to fight at all. While they were blowing their trumpets, the enemy soldiers all attacked each other!

Who made that happen? (v22) → The _ _ _ _ _ _ _ _

PRAY

"The Lord is faithful to all His promises." Psalm 145v13

As we saw at the beginning of this page, God had <u>promised</u> to be with Gideon and to give him victory. And God did! **Thank God** that He always keeps His promises.

DAY 38 TOO PROUD?

As He had promised, God gave victory to Gideon's men. The surviving Midianites ran away, hoping to escape across the Jordan river.

So Gideon sent messengers to a group of Israelites called the Ephraimites. The Ephraimites fought the Midianites by the river, and killed two Midianite leaders, called Oreb and Zeeb. (*This is in Judges 7v22-25.*)

But the Ephraimites weren't happy...

READ
Judges 8v1

Why did you t_____ us like this? Why didn't you c_____ us when you went to fight the Midianites?

The Ephraimites were annoyed that Gideon started the fight without them. It seems that they were more interested in grabbing glory for <u>themselves</u> than for <u>God</u>!

THINK + PRAY

Are you like the Ephraimites?
Do you get **jealous** of other people? If you see someone doing things for God, or being praised for what they have done, do you wish it was <u>you</u> getting the praise instead? If you sometimes get jealous, tell God you're sorry and ask Him to help you to change.

READ
Judges 8v2-3

Gideon could have been really cross with the Ephraimites! Instead, he was polite and pointed out the good stuff they had done.

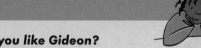

THINK + PRAY

Are you like Gideon?
What do you do when someone is angry with you? Do you shout at them? Or storm off in a huff? It's better to follow Gideon's example, and answer them politely. But that can be hard to do! So ask God to help you.

DAY 39 TOO SCARED?

Gideon and his 300 men were still chasing the rest of the Midianites, and their kings Z+Z. (*Actually, they were called Zebah and Zalmunnah—but Z+Z is easier to say!!!*)

Gideon's men were exhausted...

READ
Judges 8v4-9

Gideon went to the town of **Succoth**. What did he need for his men? (v5)

Bricks   Brushes   Brides   Bread   Briefcases

But the leaders of Succoth refused!

What did Gideon tell them? (v7)

> When the **L**_____ has handed Z+Z over to me, I will beat you with **t**_____ and **b**_____ from the desert.

 xtb Judges 8v4-21

Gideon then went to the town of **Peniel** for help. But they refused, too! What did Gideon say he would do when he returned? (v9)

> Tear down their **t**_____

Gideon **trusted God** to give him victory over Z+Z. And he was right! Later, Gideon went back to *Succoth*, and had the leaders whipped (just as he had said he would). Then he went to *Peniel*, and tore down their tower. (v10-21)

THINK + PRAY

The people in Succoth and Peniel refused to feed Gideon's men. They were **scared** that Gideon would be defeated. And then Z+Z would attack them for helping Gideon. *They didn't trust God.*

Do <u>you</u> ever chicken out of standing up for God because you're scared of what people might say or do? Ask God to give you the courage to stand up for Him, and do the right thing, even when that's hard.

DAY 40 GOOD, SAD, BAD

GOOD

Gideon had rescued the Israelites from their enemies. Now they wanted him to become their king...

READ
Judges 8v22-23

What was Gideon's answer? (v23)

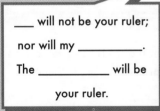

___ will not be your ruler; nor will my _____. The _____ will be your ruler.

Gideon knew that it was really **God** who had rescued the Israelites. _God was their true King._

SAD

But then Gideon did something sad...

READ
Judges 8v24-27

What did Gideon ask each person to give him? (v24)

a) An ear-ring
b) An ear-lobe
c) An ear-wig

Gideon made an ephod from the gold.
(An ephod was an item of clothing worn by priests.)

God was the _real King_. The Israelites should have worshipped <u>Him</u>. But they worshipped the gold ephod instead!

BAD

Do you remember the circle pattern in the Book of Judges?
It's on Day 21, if you're not sure.

READ
Judges 8v33-35

As soon as Gideon died, the people <u>turned away</u> from God again! They forgot that _God is the real King._

PRAY

God is the real King today, too. (_And tomorrow, and the next day, and the next..._) Ask God to help you never to forget that He is _your King_. Ask Him to help you to put Him <u>first</u> in your life, every day.

DAY 41 HEAVENLY PRAISE

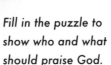
Welcome to the book of Psalms!

Psalms are songs and prayers written by God's people, the Israelites. People wrote psalms in all sorts of moods and situations—there's even one that was written in a cave! Let's start by praising God...

READ
Psalm 148v1-6

What is this psalm about?

(Circle) your answer.

Saying sorry

Asking for help

Praising God

Praising God means telling Him how <u>wonderful</u> He is.

How many times is the word "praise" used in verses 1-6?

Wow! This person really wants God to be praised!

Fill in the puzzle to show who and what should praise God.

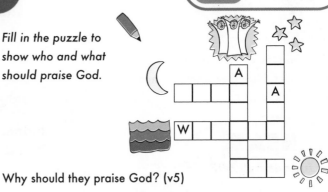

Why should they praise God? (v5)

He c r __ __ t __ d them

That means God *made* them and He's *in charge* of them for ever! No wonder they should praise Him!

THINK SPOT

The <u>stars</u> are beautiful. The <u>sun</u> is powerful. But it's **God** who should be praised. <u>He</u> made them!

PRAY
Dear God, everything in heaven should praise You! Please help <u>me</u> to praise You too. Amen

Crack the code to see where God should be praised.

— — — — — — — — — — — — —

 = E

 = H

 = R

 = V

 = W

 = Y

Everything in heaven <u>and</u> earth should praise God!

READ
Psalm 148v7-13

All the earth should praise God! Complete the pictures and write down which verse you found them in (v7-10).

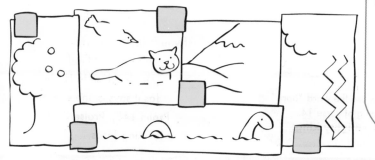

What sort of people should praise God? (v11-12)

 K_____

B_____ and G_____

O_____ people and C_____

Everyone, no matter who they are or where they come from, should praise God.
God is g_____ than anyone or anything else, and more g_____ than anything in heaven or earth! (v13)

glorious greater

Look at the picture you finished. What should everything in the picture do? P_____ G_____

PRAY

God is greater than the highest mountain, the fiercest storm, the mightiest king, and the largest whale! God is more powerful and wonderful than **anything** in heaven or earth. Join in with the rest of creation and praise Him!

DAY 43 THE PEOPLE'S PRAISE

God deserves praise from everything and everyone!
From **angels**, **sun**, **stars**, **snow**, **trees**, **birds**, **kings** and **children**.

Find these words from Psalm 148 in the wordsearch.

Who's praising God in v14?

God's people, I_____

Read around the crown to see why Israel should praise God.

God made them strong and gave them a mighty king.

Psalm 148v14

David was Israel's greatest king. BUT God promised David that an even <u>greater</u> King would come to rescue and lead His people. When this psalm was written, they were <u>still waiting</u> for that King.

Use the leftover letters (in order) from the wordsearch to see who God's great King is.

_ _ _ _ _

King Jesus came to rescue us and make us God's friends by dying on a cross. What a great King!

PRAY

If you follow Jesus, then you're one of God's people, close to His heart (as it says at the end of Psalm 148). Praise God for King Jesus.

Did You Know?

Most Bible versions use the word "horn" at the beginning of verse 14. A horn means a **mighty king!**

READ
Psalm 148v14

DAY 44 POINTLESS PLOTS

Sadly, not everyone praises God...

READ
Psalm 2v1-6

King David wrote it!

What are the kings doing? (v1-2)

☐ Praising God 🙂

☐ Plotting against God and His King (Anointed One) 🙁

What do they think they can do? (v3)

Put the gaps in the right paces.

SETTHEM SELVESFR EEFR OMGO D SCONTROL

S_____ t_____ f_____

f_____ G_____ c_____

How does David describe their plans? (v1) ✔ *your answer*

☐ They might work.   ☐ They're useless!

Is God worried about these plans? (v4-6)

☐ A little   ☐ No Way!

THINK SPOT It's <u>ridiculous</u> to think that humans can defeat God! That's like an ant thinking it can beat up an elephant! But it isn't just stupid—it's also <u>wrong</u> to rebel against God's loving, perfect rule.

Who will rule, no matter what? (v6)   **God's K_____**

> People often plotted against King David, but he knew that human plans couldn't stop God!

WAIT! Psalm 2 isn't just about David; it's also about King Jesus! People plotted against Jesus, and killed Him—but **God** was in control, and *Jesus will rule as King for ever!*

PRAY Jesus is King, no matter what people say or do. Praise God!

DAY 45 TAKE REFUGE

Follow the arrows to see what we've learned about God's King.

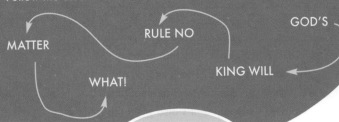

MATTER

RULE NO

GOD'S

WHAT!

KING WILL

READ
Psalm 2v7-12

• What does God call His King? (v7)   **His S_____**

• What will belong to Him? (v8)   **The n_____**

• What will His rule be like? (v9)

☐ He'll be weak and unable to punish people

☐ He'll be a powerful judge

Wow! He's God's Son; the people of the nations belong to Him; and He's a powerful judge! Only <u>one</u> King fits that description—**King Jesus!**

Remember the kings who thought they could get rid of God's King? (v1-3) They need to change their plans!

What should they do? (v11-12)

S_____ God with **f_____** and
J_____, and **r_____** His King.

respect
joy
fear
serve

Draw the rest of each dotted line to show what will happen to these people (v12).

Look after me, King Jesus!

I don't want God in charge!

Punishment and destruction

Protection and blessings

THINK SPOT

How do <u>you</u> treat King Jesus?

PRAY   Ask God to help you to love, serve and trust King Jesus.

Welcome back to the book of **Judges**.

READ
Judges 13v1

Do you remember the circle pattern in Judges?
Underline the parts that are true in verse 1.

God's people disobeyed Him.

God allowed their enemies to defeat them.

God sent a rescuer to save His people.

God's people called out to Him, saying, "Save us!"

Verse 1 was about the **purple** and **blue** parts of the circle pattern. Now we're going to meet two people—Manoah and his wife—who are an important part of the **green** section of the pattern. They have never been able to have children. But that's about to change...

READ
Judges 13v2-5

What was God's message to Manoah's wife? (v3)
    a) You will never have children.
    b) You may have a child one day.
    c) You are going to have a son.

Manoah's wife was told not to drink wine or eat forbidden food. What was her son going to be? (v5)
    a) A Narrator
    b) A Nazirite
    c) A Navigator

Turn to the next page.

Did You Know?

A **Nazirite** was someone whose whole life was set aside to serve God in a special way. He or she had to let their hair grow long, and never cut it. *You can read about Nazirites in Numbers 6v1-5.*

God said something very special about the son He was giving to Manoah and his wife. What was it? (v5)

 the correct answers.

He would **begin** / **finish** the work of **handing over** / **rescuing** the Israelites from the **Midianites** / **Philistines**.

THINK SPOT

Look back at the circle pattern on the previous page, and read the red part again.

This time, the Israelites <u>haven't</u> cried out to God to rescue them. But God still does! The message to Manoah's wife is that a *saviour will be born*. God is providing a rescuer, to save His people from their enemies, even though they haven't cried out to Him for help.

The special word for this is **grace**. Grace is God's HUGE kindness to people who don't deserve it. It's an undeserved gift. The Israelites <u>didn't deserve</u> to be rescued. They hadn't even asked God for help! But God showed His *amazing grace* by sending them a rescuer.

THINK + PRAY

Over 1000 years later, God did the same thing when He sent another baby boy to be the greatest Rescuer ever—**Jesus Christ**. God didn't send Jesus because people <u>deserved</u> it. He sent Jesus because of His *amazing grace* to us. **Thank God** for being like this.

DAY 47 ANSWERS AND PROMISES

xtb Judges 13v6-25

God has told Manoah and his wife that they'll have a son who will rescue Israel!

READ
Judges 13v8-14

Manoah wanted to know how to bring up this special baby for God. So he **asked God**. (v8)

What amazing thing happened? (v9)

> G_____ heard M_____ and sent
>
> His A_____ to visit them again.

PRAY

Wow! We sometimes forget how **amazing** prayer is. God is the wonderful, powerful Creator of the Universe. And yet He <u>listens</u> when we talk to Him, and <u>answers</u> our prayers. **Thank and praise God for this.**

Manoah and his wife prepared a sacrifice (a gift) for God. As the flame of the sacrifice blazed up high, an amazing thing happened. The <u>angel</u> went up in the flames as well!

Then Manoah and his wife realised that it was **God** they'd been talking to! (*This is in v15-23.*)

READ
Judges 13v24-25

What was the boy's name? (v24) S_____

God was with Samson, and gave him His Spirit (v25). Samson would <u>rescue</u> the Israelites just as God had said.

PRAY

God's promise to Manoah and his wife came true. They had a son, just as He had said. **Thank God** that His promises <u>always</u> come true.

DAY 48 GOD'S PERFECT PLANS

Judges 14v1-7

Samson is now grown up. God is going to use him to <u>rescue</u> the Israelites from the Philistines.

READ
Judges 14v1-4

Who did Samson want to marry?
Take the first letter of each picture.

_____

_____

Did you know?

The **Philistines** were enemies of God and His people. God had told His people <u>not</u> to marry their enemies (Deuteronomy 7v1-3). No wonder Samson's parents were upset!

Did you spot the <u>shock</u> in verse 4?

_____

_____

Samson was <u>disobeying</u> God. He should <u>not</u> marry a Philistine woman. *BUT* God was going to use this situation in His plans to rescue the Israelites.

Nothing can stop God's perfect plans!

READ
Judges 14v5-7

Who gave Samson the <u>strength</u> to kill a lion with his bare hands?

_____

_____

God's **Holy Spirit** helped Samson to kill a lion which would normally have killed him!

PRAY

God's Spirit would help Samson to rescue the Israelites, just as God had planned. **Thank God** that <u>nothing</u> can stop His perfect plans.

DAY 49 RIDDLE TIME

Samson has set off to marry a Philistine woman. On the way, he stops to look at the lion he killed...

READ
Judges 14v8-9

What did Samson find in the lion's body? (v8)

A swarm of **b**_____ and some **h**_____ .

At his wedding, Samson gave a feast for seven days. During the feast, Samson set a riddle:

Out of the eater, something to eat;
Out of the strong, something sweet.

The prize for solving the riddle would be 30 sets of fine clothing.

The Philistine guests couldn't work the riddle out, and they got angry...

They threatened Samson's wife—so she nagged him and nagged him until he told her the answer.

Then she told the rest of the Philistines!

What is sweeter than

_ _ _ _ _ _ ?

What is stronger than
a _ _ _ _ ?

When they said this, Samson knew that his wife had told them. He was very angry...

READ
Judges 14v19-20

It seems <u>unfair</u> that Samson killed these 30 men. And it seems <u>unfair</u> that someone else gets Samson's wife. **BUT...**

<u>Who</u> gave Samson the strength to kill 30 men? (v19)

The **S**_____ of the **L**_____

God was in control!

LORD   Spirit

THINK + PRAY

Samson and the Philistines now <u>hate</u> each other. The scene is set for God to use Samson to <u>rescue</u> the Israelites from the Philistines—just as God has planned. Thank God (as we did yesterday) that nothing can stop His perfect plans.

DAY 50 FOX FIRE

Does Samson seem an unlikely hero? Today, God uses Samson to defeat even more of the Philistines...

READ
Judges 15v1-5

Circle the wrong words.

At the time of the thistle harvest, Samson took flowers and went to visit his wife. But her mother would not let Samson go in, because Samson's wife had been given to his servant. Samson said that he would harm the Philippians as a result. He caught 500 badgers, and tied them tail to nose in pairs. Then he fastened a banana to every pair of tails. Samson lit the torches, and set them loose in the towns of the Philistines, to burn up their televisions.

Answers: thistle, flowers, mother, servant, Philippians, 500, badgers, nose, banana, towns, televisions.

The **Philistines** were angry about their burnt crops. So they murdered Samson's wife and her father. That made **Samson** furious, too. So he attacked and killed many Philistines. (v6-8)

THINK SPOT

Today's story is difficult. There's so much *anger* and *killing*. (There will be tomorrow as well.) But we need to remember what **God said** before Samson was born:

Cross out the X's

He will **XBXEXGIXNX** the work of **XRXESXCXUIXNXGX** the Israelites from the **XPHXIXLIXSTXIXNEXSX**.

Judges 13v5

The Philistines were the **enemies** of God and His people. So God was using Samson to <u>defeat</u> the Philistines, and <u>rescue</u> the Israelites from them.

THINK + PRAY

God is always in control, even in difficult situations. His plans always work out. **Thank God** that He is in control. **Ask Him** to help you to trust Him, even when things are difficult.

DAY 51 — JAW-BONE HILL

The <u>Philistines</u> are out to get Samson. And the <u>Israelites</u> have agreed to help! 3000 Israelites (from the tribe of Judah) have gone to get Samson, and hand him over to the Philistines...

READ
Judges 15v12-17

What was Samson tied up with? (v13)

Two _____

The ropes were new and strong—but when the Philistines rushed towards Samson, the ropes became as weak as burnt plants! (v14)

Suddenly, Samson was **free**—and ready to **fight**!

What did Samson use as a weapon? (v15)

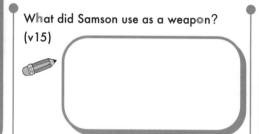

Samson was very strong, but <u>who</u> gave him the power to kill 1000 Philistines? (v14)

The **S**_____ of the **L**_____

Spirit LORD

It was **God** who gave Samson the strength he needed!

Afterwards, Samson had another problem. He was weak and thirsty, but there was no water to drink. So Samson cried out to God for help.

Copy down the <u>red letters</u> (in order) to see what God did.

_ _ _ opened up a

_ _ _ _ _ _ _ place in the

ground, and _ _ _ _ _ _

came out of it.

(This is in v18-20.)

THINK + PRAY

Samson is the strongest man in the Bible. But he still needed to *turn to God for help*. That's true for you and me, too. If you have a <u>problem</u> you're worried about, or if you want to <u>serve God</u> but you find it hard, then *turn to God for help*. Talk to Him now...

DAY 52 HERO GETS ZERO

We've seen that Samson is a strong **hero**. But today he scores **zero** by disobeying God...

Samson went to Gaza, where he saw a woman he fancied. So he went to bed with her, even though they weren't married. He **disobeyed** God's laws. Zero for the hero!

The Philistines heard where Samson was and tried to trap him in the city. But Samson escaped, and carried away the city gates on his shoulders! *Still a strong hero!*

But next, Samson fell for a girl called **Delilah**...

READ
Judges 16v4-6

Samson's enemies went to Delilah and offered her loads of money to betray him. So Delilah <u>begged</u> Samson to tell her the secret of his great strength.

Read round the pics to see three things he told her.

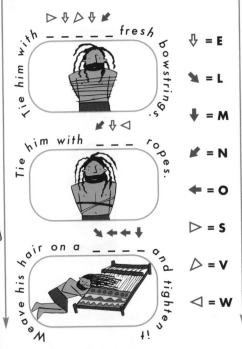

Tie him with fresh bowstrings.

Tie him with ___ ropes.

Weave his hair on a ___ and tighten it!

⇩ = E
↘ = L
↓ = M
↗ = N
← = O
▷ = S
△ = V
◁ = W

Each time, Delilah did what Samson had said. But it didn't work. Samson was still as strong as ever.

Tomorrow we'll find out what happens when Delilah keeps on nagging...

THINK+PRAY

Samson's strength came from **God**, so that Samson could *rescue* the Israelites from the Philistines. And the <u>sign</u> of it was that Samson had never cut his hair (which he mustn't tell Delilah!). But today we've seen Samson <u>disobeying</u> God, and tomorrow it will get worse. Samson is <u>not</u> living the way God wants him to. Even a "hero" like Samson can get zero when it comes to obeying God.

How about you? Are you living for God? Or have you let Him down? If you have disobeyed God, tell Him you're sorry and ask Him to help you to change.

HAIR TODAY, GONE TOMORROW

 Judges 16v16-22

Please tell me what you're worried about. I promise I won't laugh.

Guess what Ann's upset about! It's **so** funny...

Poor Ann! She told Sarah her secret, and now everybody knows about it!

Samson had a secret too—the secret of his strength...

Did you know?

Samson was a **Nazirite**. He was set apart to serve God, and put God <u>first</u> in everything. He showed this by never cutting his hair. God gave Samson amazing strength. **But** if his hair was ever cut, Samson would no longer be an obedient Nazirite. And God would no longer give him great strength.

Delilah has been nagging and nagging Samson to tell her his secret. Do you think he'll give in?

READ
Judges 16v16-20

Did Samson tell Delilah his secret? (v18)   **Yes / No**

Who shaved Samson's head? (v19)
Delilah / a man / Samson

With short hair, Samson's strength left him. But something far worse happened too (v20). *Read round the spiral to see what it was.*

that the LORD had left him. He did not know

READ
Judges 16v21-22

The Philistines put Samson to work in a prison. But what began to happen? (v22)

The Philistines think it's all over—and that <u>they've</u> won. But they've forgotten that **God** is the one who's really in control...

PRAY

Samson was supposed to put <u>God</u> first in his life. But instead he put <u>Delilah</u> first! Do **you** put God first in the way you live your life? Talk to Him about your answer.

Samson has been captured and blinded by the Philistines. He's now working in their prison. It looks like it's all over for God's hero...

READ
Judges 16v23-25

What were the Philistines saying? (v23)

> Our **g**_____ has given us victory over our enemy,
>
> **s**_____.

They thought that their pretend god, called Dagon, had won. But they were wrong! The **One True God** was <u>always</u> in control...

The **Philistines** called for Samson to be brought to their temple. 3000 Philistines were on the temple **roof**, watching as Samson came in. Their **kings** were there too. Samson stood in the middle of the temple, leaning on two **pillars**.

Then Samson **prayed** to **God**, "O LORD, remember me. Please give me **strength** just once more." Then Samson **pushed** against the pillars with all his strength. The temple fell down, killing the Philistines and their kings. **Samson** was killed, too. (v25-31)

Fit all of the blue words into the puzzle.

G _ _ _ _ _ _ _

PRAY

The Philistines thought their pretend god had won. But they were wrong! **God** is the real King! He is <u>always</u> in control. His plans <u>always</u> work out. **Thank God** for being like this.

DAY 55 GOD'S HERO

The death of God's hero...

- **Samson** was sent by God to **rescue** the Israelites from the Philistines. (Day 46)
- **God** gave Samson great **strength**. (Day 48)
- But Samson **disobeyed** God—so God left him. (Day 53)
- Later, when Samson prayed to God again, God gave him the strength to **destroy** the Philistine temple. (Day 54)

READ
Judges 16v31

How long had Samson been Israel's leader (Judge) for? _____ years

Find all of the <u>blue</u> words in the wordsearch. (Some are written backwards.)

J	E	N	O	S	M	A	S	S	U
R	E	S	C	U	E	G	O	D	S
C	D	I	S	O	B	E	Y	E	D
H	R	I	Y	O	R	T	S	E	D
S	T	R	E	N	G	T	H	S	T

The death of God's HERO!

God did use Samson to begin to rescue the Israelites from the Philistines, just as He had promised. But Samson was a <u>disobedient</u> hero.

Copy the leftover letters from the wordsearch (in order) to find God's perfect Hero.

 _ _ _ _ _ _ _ _ _ _ _ _

Jesus is our perfect Hero!

- He lived a **perfect life**. Unlike Samson, Jesus <u>never</u> disobeyed God.
- He **died** on the cross, to take the punishment for our sins, so that if we believe in Him we can be forgiven.
- But Jesus didn't stay dead! He came **back to life** again, and is still alive today, in heaven.

PRAY

Thank God for sending Jesus, our perfect Hero, to rescue us from our sins.

For a free copy of a booklet called *"Why Did Jesus Die?"*, <u>write to</u> XTB, The Good Book Company, Blenheim House, 1 Blenheim Road, Epsom, Surrey, KT19 9AP, UK <u>or email me</u> at alison@thegoodbook.co.uk

DAY 56 MEET RUTH

The story of **Ruth** is set in the time of the **Judges**.

Remember that there was a <u>pattern</u> that kept being repeated through these times.

God's people disobeyed Him.

God allowed their enemies to defeat them.

God's people called out to Him, saying, "Save us!"

God sent a rescuer to save His people.

The time of the Judges lasted for about 400 years.

Cross out the X's to find out what things were like in Israel at that time.

EXVEXXRXYXXOXNXXEX

XDXXIDXJXXUXSXXTXAXXSX

HXEXPLXXEXASXXEXDX

E _ _ _ _ _ _ _ _

_ _ _ _ _ _ _ _

_ _ _ _ _ _ _

Judges 21v25

Draw lines to match up who's *in charge of what...*

Assembly   Referee

Football match   Headteacher

America   Your teacher

Your class   President

Who do you think is *in charge* when things seem to go <u>wrong</u>?

Think carefully...

...then turn to the next page to find out more about the story of Ruth.

WHO'S IN CHARGE?

xtb — Ruth 1v1-5

READ
Ruth 1v1-5

✔ your answers.

Where did Elimelech and his family come from? (v2)

	Jerusalem
	Bethlehem
	Moab

Why did they leave? (v1)

	for a family reunion
	to go to a festival
	because of a famine

Where did they go? (v1)

	Manchester
	Moab
	Melbourne

Did You know?

The people of Moab <u>didn't</u> follow **God** and His ways. Instead, they worshipped other gods.

Elimelech's decision to take his family to Moab was a **bad choice**.

Fill in the names on the family tree.

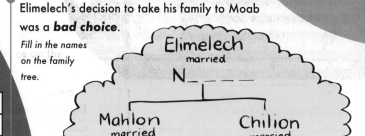

Elimelech married N _ _ _ _ _

Mahlon married R _ _ _ _ _

Chilion married O _ _ _ _

Mahlon and Chilion married girls from Moab who <u>didn't</u> follow God. That was a **bad choice**.

Three sad things happened to this family in Moab. Which three people died? Circle their names.

Elimelech   Naomi   Mahlon   Chilion   Orpah   Ruth

It looks like this family have made some bad choices. Things are very hard for them. But as we'll see, **God** is still in charge.

PRAY
Thank God that He is in charge even when things are hard.

DAY 57 TRUSTING IN GOD

xtb Ruth 1v6-22

Naomi hears that there is food in Bethlehem. (The famine is over.)

Naomi, Ruth and Orpah get ready to leave Moab.

Naomi tells Ruth and Orpah they should stay in Moab with their mothers.

Ruth and Orpah start crying. They want to stay with Naomi.

Match up the jigsaw pieces to find out what Ruth said.

READ
Ruth 1v15-18

Finally, Orpah kisses Naomi goodbye, and goes back.

Wherever you go	will be my God
Wherever you live	will be my people
Your people	I will live
Your God	I will go

Even though Ruth came from a country that didn't follow God, she had learned about God. She has put her trust in God and become part of God's family.

PRAY

Thank God that <u>anyone</u> can become part of His family. Have you put your trust in God?

DAY 58 A GODLY MAN

Use these words to fill in the gaps and find out one of **God's instructions** in the book of *Leviticus*.

ears   corn

fields   harvest

back   poor

When you **h**_____ your

f_____ do not cut the

c_____ at the edges of the fields,

and do not go **b**_____ to cut the

e_____ of corn that were left.

Leave them for the **p**_____.

Leviticus 19v9-10

Today we're going to find out about someone who followed God's instructions.

1. Naomi had a relative called Boaz.

2. As it turned out, Ruth went into <u>his</u> fields to gather corn.

3. Ruth went behind the harvesters picking up what was left.

4. Boaz arrived and asked the man in charge who Ruth was.

5. Boaz told Ruth to help herself to a drink.

6. Ruth asked him, "Why are you concerned about me?"

READ
Ruth 2v11-13

Take the first letter of each pic.

- Boaz had heard about Ruth's

kindness to __ __ __ __

- Boaz shows great

__ __ __ __ __ __ __ __ __ to Ruth.

Remember what things were like in the times of the Judges? —"everyone did just as he pleased". But **Boaz** is a godly man, following God's instructions.

PRAY

Thank God for someone you know who is a godly person, who follows God's instructions.

DAY 59 GREAT KINDNESS

xtb Ruth 2v14-23

Draw what was left on your plate after dinner yesterday.

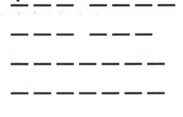

God's law said that Boaz should leave the leftovers for people like Ruth. *(That means leftovers in his field of corn—not a few cold peas or sprouts!)*
But Boaz does <u>more</u> than that...

READ
Ruth 2v14-16

How does Boaz show great kindness to Ruth?

• he gave her _____ to eat (v14)

• he told his men to leave _____

for her to pick up (v16).

Ruth went home with <u>loads</u> of corn!

In a field belonging to Boaz.

Where did you gather corn today?

Follow the arrow to find out what Naomi said.

→	T	H	E	L	O
E	D	S	H	O	R
P	D	N	E	W	D
P	N	S	S	I	H
O	I	K	G	N	A
T	S	T	O	N	S

T ___ ___   ___ ___ ___ ___

___ ___ ___   ___ ___ ___

___ ___ ___ ___ ___ ___

___ ___ ___ ___   ___

___ ___ ___ ___ ___

Ruth 2v20

<u>Boaz</u> had shown great kindness to Ruth. But Naomi saw that **God** was the one looking after them.

PRAY

Think about some of the ways God looks after you and shows you kindness. Then say **thank you** to Him.

DAY 60 FAMILY MATTERS

How many cousins do you have?

Write their names here:

THINK SPOT

If your cousin was having a bad time, would you help them, or say that it serves them right?

Did You Know?

In Israel, if your cousin Dan was having a bad time, or lost his job, or short of cash, or... you couldn't just say "serves him right". As a relative you <u>had</u> to help.
- If he needed to sell a field to get some money—you could <u>buy back</u> (or *redeem*) the field for him.
- If he died without having any sons (to carry on the family name) —you could <u>marry</u> his wife, and any sons born would count as Dan's sons.

If you did this, you were known as a

➔ ↑ ↘ ▷ ↓ ⇧ ↘   ▽ ⇩ ↘ ↓ ↓ ↓ ↓ ⇧ ▽

_ _ _ _ _ _ _   _ _ _ _ _ _ _

Arrow Code

⇧ = A
↘ = D
⇩ = E
↑ = I
➔ = K
↓ = M
↘ = N
▽ = R
▷ = S

Look back to Day 56. Which three people died?

E_____

M_____ C_____

Naomi has <u>no husband</u>, and <u>no sons</u>. She needs a *Kinsman–Redeemer*. Naomi is too old to have any more children herself. But, if a Kinsman-Redeemer married Ruth and had a son, he would count as Elimelech and Naomi's son.

READ
Ruth 2v20

Who is a close relative, and Kinsman–Redeemer of Naomi and Ruth?

PRAY

It wasn't a mistake that Ruth ended up working in Boaz's field. God arranged it that way! **Thank God** that He is always in control.

WEDDING BELLE?

AT HOME

Naomi wants to find a husband for Ruth. She tells Ruth to wash and put on her best clothes and perfume, and then go to the threshing floor where Boaz will be. (*That's where they beat the grain off the barley plants.*)

THRESHING FLOOR

Ruth does what Naomi says. When Boaz has finished eating, Ruth lies down at his feet.

READ
Ruth 3v8-13

IN THE NIGHT

Use these words to fill in the gaps.

care   marry   Naomi   trust

It might seem an odd way to do it, but Ruth was asking Boaz to

m_____ her! Boaz is

someone she can **t**_____ to

take **c**_____ of her and

N_____.

It looks like there might be a wedding... but what does v12 say?

There is a _ _ _ _ _ _ _ _

_ _ _ _ _ _ _ _ _ _

who is a <u>closer</u> relative than Boaz.

AT HOME

Ruth tells Naomi everything (v14-18). *Cross out the X's to find out what Naomi said.*
BXEXX
PXAXTXIXEXNXT

THINK + PRAY

Naomi tells Ruth to be patient, and to keep trusting God. Are <u>you</u> good at trusting God, even when problems appear? Talk to God about your answer.

DAY 62 WITH THIS SANDAL...

xtb Ruth 4v1-12

What do you take out of your pocket when you buy something?

coins credit card cheque sandal £10 note

Did you know?

In the time of Ruth, taking off your sandal was like signing an agreement! The deal was done when you took your sandal off.

Ruth has asked Boaz to marry her.

But remember that there is another Kinsman-Redeemer. So Boaz goes to the town gate to talk to him.

At first the other man wants to buy back (*redeem*) the land that belonged to Naomi's husband, Elimelech.

But when he realises that he will have to take care of Ruth and Naomi as well, he changes his mind.

READ
Ruth 4v8-12

Boaz bought (or *redeemed*) everything that had belonged to Elimelech.

Who became his wife? (v10)

Boaz has carried out his duty as **Kinsman-Redeemer**.

At the town gate, people prayed for God to bless Boaz and Ruth. They prayed that:

• Ruth would be like **R_____** and **L_____** (they both had lots of children).

• Boaz would be **f_____** in Bethlehem.

• Their family would be like the family of **P_____** (an important family).

PRAY Pray for anyone you know who has just got married, or will be marrying soon. Ask God to help them love each other, and love and serve Him together.

DAY 63 FAITHFUL ONE

 Ruth 4v13-17

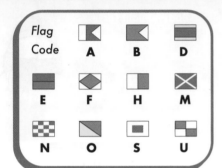

Flag Code

A B D
E F H M
N O S U

Back in chapter one, Naomi had prayed that God would give both

Ruth and Orpah a _ _ _ _

and a _ _ _ _ _ _ .

You can check out Naomi's prayer in Ruth 1v9.

READ
Ruth 4v13-17

(Circle) the correct words.

Boaz took Ruth home as his **widow / wife / servant**.

She gave birth to **twins / a daughter / a son**.

The child was named **Obed / Orpah / David**.

Starting with **P**, fill in every <u>second</u> letter below to find out what the women said when Ruth had a son.

P _ _ _ _

_ _ _ _ _ _ (v14)

THINK SPOT

At the start of Chapter One, things didn't look good for Naomi. Her husband died and her two sons died. It looked unlikely that Elimelech's family line would carry on.

BUT this son *Obed*, who was born to Boaz and Ruth, counts as Elimelech and Naomi's son!

God has shown great faithfulness to Naomi and Ruth.

PRAY

God is always faithful. That means we can always trust Him, and that He always keeps His promises. Thank God for being like this.

Ruth 4v17-22

Have you ever met the Queen?

Do you have any famous relatives?

Today we're going to discover some **royal** connections.

READ
Ruth 4v17-22

What was Boaz and Ruth's son called? (v17)

What was Obed's son called? (v17)

What was Jesse's son called? (v17)

That's **King David**—the famous King of Israel!

Use yesterday's flag code.

Back in verse 11, the elders prayed that Boaz would be __ __ __ __ __ .

In verse 14 the women prayed that Obed would be __ __ __ __ __ __ too.

Those prayers were answered! **Boaz** became the great grandfather of King David. And **Obed** became the grandfather of King David.

All through the story of Ruth, God has been working out His big plan. He chose Ruth, the foreigner from Moab, to be the great grandmother of the greatest king Israel ever had—King David! (And, as we'll see tomorrow, someone even greater than David came from Ruth's family as well.)

PRAY

Thank God that He uses ordinary people—like Ruth, and like you and me!—to work out His plans.

What are the names of your grandparents?

Do you know the names of your great grandparents?

Yesterday we found out that **Boaz** and **Ruth** were the great grandparents of K_____ D_____.

Today we're going to jump forward to the very beginning of the book of Matthew. It starts with a family tree (sometimes called a "genealogy"). Look out for some names from the story of Ruth as you read it.

READ
Matthew 1v1-6 & 16

Did you spot some familiar names?

Eventually the family line of Boaz and Ruth leads to

J_____ C_____

Naomi and Ruth needed someone to **rescue** them, to make their future safe and secure.

God provided **Boaz**, to be their **Kinsman-Redeemer**.

We <u>all</u> need someone to **rescue** us from sin and God's judgment to make our future safe and secure.

God provided **Jesus**, to be our **Redeemer** and Rescuer.

*If you're not sure how Jesus redeems (buys back) and rescues us, then check back to **The Servant King** after Day 13.*

PRAY Thank God for sending Jesus to be our Redeemer and Rescuer.

TIME FOR MORE?

Have you read all 65 days of XTB?
Well done if you have!

How often do you use XTB?
- Every day?
- Nearly every day?
- Two or three times a week?
- Now and then?

You can use XTB at any time...

In the morning.

At bedtime.

When you get back from school.

When do <u>you</u> read XTB?

XTB comes out every three months. If you've been using it every day, or nearly every day, that's great! You may still have a few weeks to wait before you get the next issue of XTB. But don't worry!—that's what the extra readings are for...

EXTRA READINGS

The next four pages contain extra Bible readings to look at some things Jesus said. If you read one each day, they will take you 26 days. Or you may want to read two or three each day. Or just pick a few to try. Whichever suits you best. There's a cracking wordsearch to solve too...

The extra readings start on the next page

Drop us a line...

Why not write in and tell us what you think of XTB:

—What do you like best?
—Was there something you didn't understand?
—And any ideas for how we can make it better!

Write to: XTB, The Good Book Company, Blenheim House, 1 Blenheim Road, Epsom, Surrey, KT19 9AP, UK **or e-mail me:** alison@thegoodbook.co.uk

WHAT JESUS SAID...

These extra readings come from several different books in the New Testament part of the Bible. Each one looks at something that **Jesus** said.

The Bible is <u>full</u> of things Jesus said! We can only look at a few of them here, so we're going to discover what He said about Himself—**who** He is, **why** He came, and the things He said while dying on the **cross**.

The ideas in the box will help you as you read the verses.

PRAY	Ask God to help you to understand what you read.
READ	Read the Bible verses, and fill in the missing word in the puzzle.
THINK	Think about what you have just read. Try to work out one main thing the writer is saying.
PRAY	Thank God for what you have learned about Him.

There are 26 Bible readings on the next three pages. Part of each reading has been printed for you—but with a word missing. Fill in the missing words as you read the verses. Then see if you can find them all in the wordsearch below. Some are written backwards—or diagonally!

If you get stuck, check the answers at the end of Reading 26.

M	G	O	D	M	E	N	P	A	R	A	D	I	S	E
O	O	T	H	E	G	B	R	E	A	D	A	P	E	T
D	O	T	R	B	I	B	E	L	I	E	V	E	R	Z
G	D	H	H	A	V	E	P	I	C	K	S	A	V	E
N	T	I	M	E	E	T	A	G	A	T	E	L	E	T
I	S	R	O	A	R	S	R	H	D	R	E	A	M	V
K	O	S	H	O	R	T	E	T	E	R	N	A	L	I
I	O	T	R	E	S	U	R	R	E	C	T	I	O	N
T	N	Y	H	T	A	B	L	E	T	A	L	K	I	E
F	A	T	H	E	R	S	B	E	L	I	E	V	E	S
B	A	L	W	A	Y	S	X	T	B	Y	A	W	A	Y
F	I	N	I	S	H	E	D	E	V	I	G	R	O	F

What Jesus said about <u>why</u> He came

Tick the box when you have read the verses.

1 ☐ **Read Mark 1v14-15**

Jesus told people the <u>good news</u>—He had come as God's promised King.

"The k _ _ _ _ _ of God is near. Turn away from your sins and believe the good news!" (v15)

2 ☐ **Read John 3v16**

Jesus came as our Rescuer, so that everyone who puts their trust in Jesus can live with Him for ever in heaven.

"For God loved the world so much that He gave His only Son, so that everyone who b _ _ _ _ _ _ _ in Him may not die but have eternal life." (v16)

3 ☐ **Read Luke 19v1-10**

Jesus sometimes called Himself "the Son of Man". He said that He came to look for and rescue lost people.

"The Son of Man came to seek and to s _ _ _ the lost." (v10)

4 ☐ **Read Mark 10v42-45**

Jesus came to serve people, and to die as our ransom (which means paying the cost to rescue us).

"The Son of Man did not come to be served, but to s _ _ _ _ , and to give His life as a ransom for many." (v45)

5 ☐ **Read John 5v24**

Jesus came to rescue people who believe in Him.

"Whoever hears my words and believes Him who sent me has e _ _ _ _ _ _ _ life." (v24)

6 ☐ **Read Mark 8v31-33**

Jesus told His followers that He would suffer and die—but then come back to life again!

"He will be put to death, but t _ _ _ _ days later He will rise to life." (v31)

The "I AM" sayings—when Jesus said "I am..."

7 ☐ **Read John 6v32-35**

Jesus is like bread that gives eternal life.

"I am the b _ _ _ _ of life." (v35)

8 ☐ **Read John 8v12**

The devil wants people to be lost in darkness—without God. But Jesus brings light!

"I am the L _ _ _ _ of the world." (v12)

9 ☐ **Read John 10v7-10**

Jesus is like a gate or door. He is the only way to be rescued from our sins and live for ever in heaven.

"I am the g _ _ _ . Whoever enters by me will be saved." (v9)

10 ☐ **Read John 10v11-15**

Jesus is like a perfect shepherd. He loves His sheep (His people), and even dies to rescue them!

"I am the **g** _ _ _ shepherd." (v11)

11 ☐ **Read John 11v25-26**

Jesus is the only one who gives eternal life. If someone who believes in Jesus dies, he will be raised to life again. This is called resurrection.

"I am the

r _ _ _ _ _ _ _ _ _ _

and the life." (v25)

12 ☐ **Read John 14v5-6**

Jesus is the <u>only</u> way to be right with God, and to live with Him forever in heaven.

"I am the **W** _ _ , the truth and the life. No one comes to the Father except through me." (v6)

13 ☐ **Read John 15v1-5**

Followers of Jesus grow to live the way He wants them to—like branches on a vine grow fruit.

"I am the **V** _ _ _ , and you are the branches." (v5)

Words Jesus spoke when He was on the cross

14 ☐ **Read Mark 15v33-39**

When Jesus died, He was cut off from God, His Father, for the very first time.

"Jesus cried out in a loud voice, 'My **G** _ _ , my God, why have you forsaken me?'" (v34)

15 ☐ **Read Luke 23v33-34**

While Jesus was being crucified, He prayed for the people who did it.

"Jesus said, '**F** _ _ _ _ _ _ them, Father. They don't know what they are doing.'" (v34)

16 ☐ **Read Luke 23v39-43**

Two thieves were killed with Jesus. One laughed at Jesus, but the other believed that Jesus was the promised King.

"Jesus said to him, 'I promise you that today you will be in

P _ _ _ _ _ _ _ with me.'" (v43)

17 ☐ **Read Luke 23v44-46**

Just before He died, Jesus prayed to God, His Father.

"Jesus cried out in a loud voice, '**F** _ _ _ _ _ , in your hands I place my spirit.'" (v46)

18 ☐ **Read John 19v25-27**

Jesus' mother Mary watched Him dying on the cross. Jesus asked His disciple, John, to take care of her.

"Jesus said to His mother, 'He is your son,' and to the disciple, 'Here is your **M** _ _ _ _ _ .'" (v26-27)

19 ☐ **Read John 19v28-29**

Jesus spoke again, so that everything the Old Testament said about Him would come true.

"Jesus said, 'I am t _ _ _ _ _ _.'" (v28)

20 ☐ **Read John 19v30**

When Jesus died, He had finished taking the punishment for our sins. He had done everything that was needed.

"Jesus said, 'It is f _ _ _ _ _ _ _.'" (v30)

Some other things Jesus said

21 ☐ **Read Luke 2v41-52**

When Jesus was 12, He was separated from Mary and Joseph. They found Him in the temple—"His Father's house".

"Didn't you know that I had to be in my F _ _ _ _ _ ' _ house?" (v49)

22 ☐ **Read Acts 20v35**

Jesus said that it is better to <u>give</u> things, than to <u>get</u> them!

"It is more blessed to g _ _ _ than to receive." (v35)

23 ☐ **Read John 14v8-11**

How can we know what God is like? By looking at Jesus!

"Anyone who has seen me, has s _ _ _ the Father." (v9)

24 ☐ **Read Matthew 28v16-20**

Jesus told His followers to tell others about Him, and He promised to always be with them.

"I will be with you a _ _ _ _ _ _ , to the end of the age." (v20)

25 ☐ **Read John 14v1-3**

Jesus promises to prepare a place in heaven for those who follow Him.

"I am going to p _ _ _ _ _ _ _ a place for you." (v2)

26 ☐ **Read Revelation 22v12-13**

At the very end of the Bible, Jesus says that He will be coming back soon.

"I am coming S _ _ _ !" (v12)

WHAT NEXT?

XTB comes out every three months. Each issue contains 65 full XTB pages, plus 26 days of extra readings. By the time you've used them all, the next issue of XTB will be available.

ISSUE EIGHT OF XTB

Issue Eight of XTB explores the books of Mark and 1 Samuel, and dips into some Psalms as well.

- The Gospel of **Mark** tells us <u>who</u> Jesus is and <u>why</u> He came. Investigate the first Easter in the last part of Mark's book about Jesus.
- Meet the last of the judges—*Samuel*—and the first king of Israel—*Saul*—in the book of **1 Samuel**.

Look out for these three seasonal editions of XTB:
Christmas Unpacked, Easter Unscrambled and *Summer Signposts*.

All available from:
UK: www.thegoodbook.co.uk
North America: www.thegoodbook.com
Australia: www.thegoodbook.com.au
New Zealand: www.thegoodbook.co.nz

XTB Joke Page

How do cockerels tell off their children?
Cock-a-doodle-don't!

Why could no one phone the zoo?
Because the lion was busy.

Where do you send a poorly horse?
To the horspital!

Where do giraffes go to do their lessons?
High school!

Two parrots are sitting on a perch. One said to the other, "I smell fish!"

Do <u>you</u> know any good jokes?
—send them in and they might appear in XTB!

Do you have any questions?
...about anything you've read in XTB.
—send them in and we'll do our best to answer them.

Write to: XTB, The Good Book Company, Blenheim House, 1 Blenheim Road, Epsom, Surrey, KT19 9AP, UK **or e-mail me:** alison@thegoodbook.co.uk